I0212792

Also by Brady Snow

Novels

The Set Sun Blood at Dusk

Poet for Hire

Non-Fiction

What's my Nitch? – My Quest for Purpose in the Content
Creator Economy

Guided Journal

Your Cosmic To-Do List: A Guided Journal for Aligning Your
Life With What Truly Matters

Newsletter

Lore of the Soul - subscribe for updates and reflections on
soulful living at bradysnow.com/newsletter

Whats my Nitch?

My Quest for Purpose in the

Content Creator Economy

by Brady Snow

WestStorm Studio

© Brady Snow, 2025
 All rights reserved.
 Printed in the United States of America

ISBN: 978-8-9931837-0-1

The author used artificial intelligence tools as part of the
creative process for editing and organizing this work. These
tools were used only as aids; the ideas, stories, and final
manuscript remain the original work of the author.

No part of this book may be reproduced, stored in a retrieval
system, or transmitted in any form or by any means —
electronic, mechanical, photocopying, recording, or otherwise
— including use in datasets for training artificial intelligence
systems — without the prior written permission of the author.

To all seekers of purpose.

May these words help you remember your voice and embody
your soul's calling.

Preface

Stranded in the Desert of Nicheless Souls

I sit defeated against the hood of my broken Toyota Sequoia in a barren desert basin in the middle of Nevada. Everything I had tried to get it to run did not work. I stopped here to shoot a video en route back home to Colorado from a California road trip.

Beside my vehicle there is a rusty abandoned car shot up with bullet holes. It looks like it has been here at least 20 years. Maybe more. I wonder if my Toyota will succumb to the same fate and if my skeleton will lay alongside both cars.

I look out at the desert landscape. Not a tree, blade of grass, or source of water in sight. Tan mountains dominate my horizon a few miles to the West. The dry ground of the basin used to be a lake bed thousands of years ago. Now only mirages tease a hint of water in this desolate land. There are further mountains in every direction. Dust devils whip sand in the basin to my South. Beyond the dust devils a vaster dustcloud gathers, threatening to blow a dust storm in upon me.

The road I drove in on is dirt. No other cars move upon it. I cannot see the paved highway that is my safe return to civilization. Few cars had been on it. I thought it was a good idea to pull off onto a side road to find a scenic spot to shoot some videos for my YouTube channel. I had been promised by 'make money online gurus' that YouTube videos were the ticket to earning more and working less.

I had recorded a video here a month prior on my way out to California to film a friend's wild horse photography workshop. I had gotten the all-inclusive food, tent, and my own horse deal for documenting the trip and making a promotional video for the program.

Since I had the gear and was taking a cool trip, I decided I might as well get my YouTube channel launched too. The topic of the video I shot here at this abandoned and bullet-ridden body of a car a month ago was about how to use your film gear. It was a scrappy video shot primarily in wide angles to capture the landscape.

Wide angles of your speaker are not favorable for viewer retention on Youtube but the landscape was very important to me. I wanted to show the absurdity of being a video tips guy within a vast and barren desert basin. Kind of like how the echo chamber of regurgitated and repetitive content in crowded niches on Youtube seemed to me.

I dropped ten grand on gear I thought I needed — partly for a wild horse gig, partly because the internet told me this was how you escaped the 9–5. The gurus promised freedom: niche down, post often, make money in your sleep. What they didn't teach was how to stay true to yourself while doing it. So I became the character they modeled. The advice guy, the self-made expert, figuring it out on camera while pretending I already had. I mimicked the blueprint while questioning the blueprint.

I had been working my flexible 9-5 remotely on the trip from cafes, hotels, and friends' places when I wasn't on the wild horse excursion. It was a content director role at a small tech company where the CEO was the informational expert on Youtube ads. Being the advice guy worked for him. Why couldn't it also work for me?

In between work sessions I filmed boat loads of content for my "personal brand." I was into a lot of topic, or niches as they say, which pulled my content in many directions. I was torn between making educational content that followed formulas and viral methods and my own desire to express myself without constraints.

My personal brand ended up with me acting as a fictitious version of myself. I made videos where I played the advice guy giving tutorials and narrating vlogs, all while being scrappy and playful. I guess I was trying to show through example that you just had to put yourself out there to get started.

The paths to monetization were many and confusing. Courses, coaching, channel monetization, affiliate deals. Everyone had a system. I felt like I had to repress my natural voice to follow the systems that promised success.

The methods that invaded my world the most at the time seemed more often than not slanted towards helping people with their personal brand or their own online business. It made sense that helping people make money was lucrative but making content in the same way thousands of others made content did not feel fulfilling. It was not manufacturing content, not creating art.

The gurus had told me you need to grow an audience first but if you followed their methods and were consistent you could monetize fast, in even as little as 3 months or less.

I of course was all in on buying the hope of this promise. I had ordered the film gear and started creating videos for YouTube and vertical videos for Instagram reels, Tikky Toks, and YouTube Shorts.

The content ended up as a freak hybrid mix of vlogging and scrappy videography education. It was no content creator cult that any sane person would follow. Yet it was the path I had to walk to reconnect with my creative expression that I had let crumble away the last few years. The truth was I was still learning video as a tool myself. I had the basics down but was by no means an expert.

I shot video for work when I was in person with the CEO of the company I worked for. We made YouTube videos, YouTube ads, trainings, and webinars, and I edited it all and reformatted all of them into vertical shorts for repurposing on social media. We were a small company but the basics of video supported our video-centric strategy to sell over 5 million dollars in software subscriptions, courses, affiliate offers, and coaching programs.

I thought if I could do it for work, and my boss could improvise the content for our YouTube videos and ads on the spot, then I could pull this off too. I just had to find my niche then create content. Only I did it in the reverse order. I created content while trying to find my niche.

I became a self-declared content creator. One swayed by the influences of other influencers all while acting as the influencer of others myself. I became an expert of influencer mimicry with my own personal twist of acting as the incompetent content creator. This was all just to keep it real. I played the role of an aspiring influencer who wasn't sure what he was really doing.

I had driven across the West from the inner Colorado Rockies to the Sierra Nevada Mountains of California and out to the Coast to shoot as much content as I could. I mainly did it because I wanted to see the land and say hello to the Ocean after a few years of being landlocked in the interior continent.

This time at the rusted car on the bottom of the dried lake bed in the barren Nevada desert, I had come to film another video on the way back home. Now I had a broken down vehicle and had to find a way back to civilization to keep working my 9-5 that still paid my bills until I figured out my YouTube/social media/filmmaking business plans and replace my full income.

I made videos about making videos. They were educational, absurdly narrative, and fiction disguised as non-fiction. It was both scrappy video education and personal vlogging about whatever niche tickled my interests at the time. I created content hoping it would lead me to a niche. I was both the influencer and the influenced.

I was stranded in the Desert of Nicheless Souls.

I didn't have the slightest idea how to fix the Toyota or how I was going to get out of this mess I had gotten myself into. So I did what I knew best. I improvised some content for the public internet.

I set my phone on the vertical axis upon my tripod and pushed record. I sat back against the hood of my car and slouched, trying to look as defeated as possible.

I began my narration to the camera:

"My car broke down and I think this is karma for not having good instagram story etiquette. You're only supposed to post like 1 or 2 stories every 4 to 8 hours."

I had been posting full threads including 20 clips a day, stringing my adventures together.

"I don't know the rule or whatever hacks the algorithm better but I'm completely out of gas, completely out of food, completely out of water, and now I'm out of beer."

I stand up and snatch my phone off the tripod to show the interior of my engine.

"So there's this dust storm blowing in, I think like maybe the radiator hose blew and then chipped the timing belt and then I ran out of radiator fluid coolant oil shit…but I'm stranded out here where I shot a YouTube video a month ago."

I start walking away from my car out into the desert.

"I guess I'll go out here where I…"

The wind picks up, drowning out my voice and drifting a hazy dust cloud towards me.

I ramble something more and then the wind slows enough to hear my voice.

"I figured I'd go out here to try and find some water…"

The gusting wind resumes and my voice trails off into the sound of the wind blasting my camera's microphone.

As the wind intensifies, I set the camera on the tripod for the next shot. I push record and then stumble out in front of the camera. I try and walk in a straight line but my head is growing faint. My steps wobble and I stumble into the dusthaze. I fall over and my world goes black.

The vertical video I edited this scene into for social media displayed the captions:

To be continued on the next episode…

Introduction

The Age of the Personal Broadcast

Not long ago in the timeline of mortals the Gods gave human beings special rectangular devices that fit in their pockets. These devices could play music, access a databank of all the world's archived information at nearly the speed of light, and capture the images and sounds of their lives and broadcast them to the world from anywhere. These devices were called smartphones. Us homo sapiens who had survived through generations of gathering food from the land and sleeping in caves took up these new tools with delight.

In early 2025 there were approximately 7.21 billion smartphones in use in the world, accounting for roughly 87.93% of all the humans on Earth. The smart phone revolutionized the way humans lived. They affect how we communicate, receive information, process world news, shop, and socialize.

Whereas for the majority of human history we had to gather together around the fire or in the village square to engage in the essential human act of storytelling, now just about every human has the ability to be their own media producer. Anyone can video themselves, write their thoughts, share images, and put their favorite songs as the soundtrack of their life and then beam it out to the public internet.

Some of us may be old enough to remember a time before smartphones. Imagine how different your day would be without that urge to reach for your phone in your pocket anytime you get the impulse to instantly satiate a hunger for some nugget of knowledge, check what your acquaintances are up to wherever they are on planet Earth, or you just want escape from the task at hand.

Imagine how your life would look without knowing that you can share your momentary experience with your digital tribe. Some of us may refuse to imagine it because perhaps you'd simply rather die than sit with your own mind's thoughts without any outside stimulus.

The invasive effects of social media as a storytelling medium have both their positive and negative effects on us. Overconsumption of surface-level distraction content can be a means of escaping the paths we are each here to walk. Yet at the same time the right message or story can reach us when we need it most. It serves to give us the insight or inspirational boost we need to realign us with our sense of purpose and our highest calling.

The fact remains that storytelling is essential to the wellbeing of humankind. Engaging with stories activates multiple regions within the brain. These include the regions involved with language processing, emotions, and movement which cultivate empathy and understanding. Storytelling also reduces our stress levels, enhance memory and bolster emotional resilience. Stories are how we make sense of the vast range of emotions we experience as human beings.

For the majority of our species' history, storytelling was enacted through the spoken word or as symbols inscribed upon rocks or cliff faces. At some point we began orchestrating performed events like coordinated dances or theatrical performances where individuals participated as characters within the story. Later we wrote stories on paper and bound them into books. Printing technology improved. We distributed and archived more and more stories. In the more recent centuries we invented the ability to record sound, capture moving images, and now distribute and archive video and sounds digitally.

In the late 1990s and early 2000s social media sites began sprouting up and then spread like wildfire in a strong and ceaseless wind. Facebook, YouTube, Twitter, Instagram, TikTok. These platforms quickly infiltrated nearly every aspect of life, becoming the primary way stories and information are shared. Even older generations got addicted. The boomers post and share and see what their friends are up to on Facebook. Millennials post and share stories on Instagram. The newer generations stare into the blaze of moving pixels on TikTok, swiping an unlimited feed of more and more content for their consumption.

Some usage facts for context as of early 2025:

- About 5.24 billion people use social media across the planet. This is 63.9% of the global population.

- The average user engages with about 6.83 different social media platforms each month.

- Around the globe, users spend an average of 2 hours and 21 minutes of their days on social media.

If we sleep 8 hours per day then we have 16 waking hours in our day. 2 hours and 21 minutes of social media usage comes out to 13% of our waking hours spent on social media platforms. This number is much higher for the most fiercely addicted addicts. Most users consume more than they create. They hear other stories more than they tell their own tales.

Yet I wonder about the quality of these so called stories in enriching our human experience. Are they silly dance videos meant for distraction or a simple means of self-expression? One where we don't have to bear any serious vulnerability by exposing our true inner emotions? Are they someone lip-speaking a pre-recorded quote from someone else? Do these micro stories enhance the quality of our lives or dilute our sense of purpose?

My story with social media usage spans a vast array of intentions and purposes. Addictions and pursuits. For me, content creation became a method to discover meaning and integrate with what I call my life's purpose and soul-aligned living.

What follows is my attempt to map that journey and trace how, in the era of constant broadcasting, I lost and found my voice again.

Act I

Seeking Purpose in the Digital Age of Disillusionment

Chapter 1

Social Media, Young Love, and Creative Striving

My first uses of social media were in the early days of Facebook. I had no concept of using it for business purposes. It was used purely as a social networking site like the companies who made them declared them as. I mainly shared pictures on it at first and used it to browse the photos of girls I had crushes on in grade school.

In the writer phase of my 20s I posted poems on Facebook. I was in love with a Woman of Poetry who lived faraway. I used the original social media site to engage in what I called poetry jousts with her.

We posted poems that felt like responses to each other's poems. When it was apparent that we were not meant to be the hopeless romantic in me continued posting my poems of love longing there as if the power of my words could win her love. I wore my heart on my sleeve and posted my heartache on the public internet. Behind this intention my social media usage was purely for emotional processing and a desire to be heard and seen. This may be why many of us post.

During this time my creative pursuits of expression were in full force. I had wanted to be a famous film actor, a writer, a musician, a filmmaker, and also flee the grid and live in the Andes Mountains of South America and be a Shaman. The metaphysical world called to me yet I was still firmly weighted down from rapid ascension to higher states of consciousness by my own ego.

After acquiring a bachelor's degree in Spanish from Western State Colorado (AKA Wasted State) in Gunnison, CO, I worked seasonal jobs and focused on creative projects. I worked whatever minimal hours I could to pay the bills. During those years I was a hotel front desk night auditor for a hotel at the ski resort, a landscaper, a snowboard instructor, and volunteered as a Spanish interpreter for the community.

Many folks said this mountain valley was an incubator from the real world. Back then before the wild inflation and surge in rent and living expenses, you could get by on very little and live the life you wanted. I worked whatever seasonal jobs had the least amount of emotional lift and time commitments. Springs and falls I had off so I could work on my creative projects or explore the Mountains as I pleased. I spent a summer living in a cabin off the grid deep in the Mountains. I adopted a Rottweiler named Zeus from here who was being fostered by my landlord.

Zeus and I became quick friends and we hiked the West Elk Mountains around Crested Butte. Together we explored the next range across the basin to the South. These were the San Juan Mountains and they were the remains of an ancient volcanic superfield that had erupted roughly 30 million years ago.

Both ranges spoke to something primal in my soul. I began seeing the shapes of the mountain ranges as shifting pieces in my dreams. I explored these same landscapes in a different time. One where I knew dinosaurs and earlier life forms had treaded. The Landscape etched itself into my being. The lifestyle in this place allowed my imagination to expand and the heart to pump wild and free.

***

My early 20s flew by and I still hadn't left the mountains of Western Colorado to go to Los Angeles and "make it" as an actor like I had spoken of doing. Friends who knew me growing up in Milwaukee, WI had said becoming an actor in L.A. would have ruined me. I couldn't tell why they thought that at the time but I could feel the grave concern they had for my soul. So near the end of my 20s I finally got the role of a lifetime in the 40th anniversary play of the Crested Butte Mountain Theatre.

Being a young man still in his 20s, the director had thought I'd want to audition for the leading male role, Witch Boy, who tries to become human so he can marry the siren bombshell of a small Appalachian town. But I didn't want that role. I wanted to play the supporting role of Conjur Man, a 300 year old witchman who lives on a mountain. I got the role when the older local man she had wanted for it turned it down.

I grew my beard out and they whitened it with shoe polish and painted wrinkles on my face to make me look old and weathered. I paced the stage hunched over a large staff with owl feathers rising from it. When I tapped it on the floor of the set the soundman cued the audio clip of a thunderstrike. This was the role for me. I had no expectation from this play beyond the sole act of embodying this character and being seen for my contribution to the larger story.

During this era some friends and I also made short films. We wrote them, acted in them, and produced them. Over two years we made four films. We made a cult-themed sacrifice film in a golden autumn aspen grove, a western-themed suspense shootout action film set in a rock garden of some of the world's oldest stones, a black and white psychological thriller set in an underfunded insane asylum, and a satirical comedy about a vision quest in the sand dunes with a live chicken as a character that we borrowed from a friend.

We rented a theatre to debut our films locally. We used Facebook and Youtube to host the promotional materials and gather an audience. I submitted these to film festivals, convinced they would launch my filmmaking career. When all of them were rejected, I still did not doubt my creative spark but I switched my creative niche yet again. I set myself to finalizing a book I had been writing in the final years of my 20s.

At some point during these carefree years of creative expression and undeterred ambition, I was at an outdoor dinner in my mountain town with the two human beings who mated in 1985 and created me.

We were sipping house margaritas with salted rims. They were talking to me about getting out of seasonal jobs and getting a more stable job. Something with higher pay and a year round salary. Something with health insurance.

I looked them sternly in the face as if their loving concern was a threat to my creative ambition and talent. As if the mere suggestion of a different career path meant I was untalented and had nothing unique to express.

I looked them in the eyes as they had to me when they scolded me as a child.

"If I don't make it with my art in the next couple years, I will become someone you can't even recognize."

They stared back at me. There was fear in their eyes. They didn't want to cross me any further for fear of triggering me. I could not be reasoned with. Consulting me would make it worse. They saw what kind of madman they had cultivated from their very loins.

There was both excited hope and dismal fear on their faces.
They said nothing.

I smiled and sipped my margarita that they had bought for me.

***

As my 20s drew to a close, the Crested Butte Film Tribe disbanded from creative power struggles and our own personal fights with our own individual employment demons. I had finally gotten a job with health insurance as a cultural liaison with the school district. I served as interpreter, translator, and bilingual teacher for two years. It wore on me though. I couldn't take not being in a creative field, so I had the principal write me a letter of recommendation to the Seattle Film Institute to go get my film school certificate.

I resigned and planned to move. Then my parents got unexpectedly divorced right as I was going through romantic struggles of my own. As strong as I portrayed myself to be when I spoke about my creative ambitions, this divorce laced with my own break ups broke me. My foundational trust in Love and support came crashing down.

I decided to forego film school to stay one more year in my mountain incubator to publish the novel I had been working on. I had spent a lot of time crafting the descriptions of this Landscape. I couldn't leave the Land where it was set until it was published. I worked at a hat shop and a booze shop to pay the bills while the writing took top priority.

That year, I published my first novel, The Set Sun Blood at Dusk, and used Facebook posts to let people know it was released. I spread the word in my community and did a few local readings. I rode the drunk bus down from the ski resort to town with a box of my books shouting "Fiction, Fiction! Get your literary fiction!"

I managed to sell perhaps 200 copies or so in total. I had studied up on self-publishing promotion but wasn't interested in spending time marketing or building up a social media following, so I began the next writing project. It was a screenplay that I told myself would be my ticket to riches and fame. In truth it was my own bizarre form of self therapy.

Its real purpose was to help me process the broken romance of the Wisconsin based lover from the Facebook-based poetry jousts. My clinging to that pain rippled out into all subsequent relationships and it made it hard for me to appreciate what I had.

Instead of crafting a narrative for audience entertainment, I took the love poems I had posted on Facebook for the lost lover and made them the poems of the protagonist in my screenplay. Since the plot was tied to my own emotional processing about the relationship and was highly personal, I started converting the script into my second novel, A Poet for Hire. I guess I had a lot more to say then the screenplay format allowed.

The novel was based off caricatures of Norse Gods and Goddesses renditioned into modern times. Since Seattle was nestled on the Puget Sound, an inland waterway of the Sea, I decided it was the closest American thing to a Scandinavian landscape where the Norse myths were formed. The novel HAD to be set there.

A year went by and a preliminary plotline of the book took shape. I finally mustered the strength to leave the mountain incubator and move. There was more to add to the novel but I had to live in the place it was set in order to complete it and make it authentic.

I got a part-time tutoring job in Seattle which was enough of an excuse for me to load up and move. The real reason I was moving was for the novel. I packed the car on a whim, strapped a single-sized mattress to the roof, covered it in a tarp, loaded up my Rottweiler, Zeus, and hit the road. I only told a few people I was leaving.

I don't remember a social media posting habit at this time. I still only had a Facebook and a Youtube and an incomplete LinkedIn profile. I had no urge to document every moment of my life at the time and only posted when I had something to share.

As the planet turned into high summer in the Northern Hemisphere, I left my mountain incubator with a car full of my belongings, my dog, and my new novel manuscript. As I left the mountain basin that had been my home for 9 years, the San Juan Mountains stood as a bastion of parapets and turrets on my southern horizon. As I left the Colorado highlands, I enter the desertlands that compose the majority of the American West.

I drove Northwest across those barren deserts and the broken ranges of the Rocky Mountains towards the Cascade Mountains and the inlet finger of the Sea.

Chapter 2

Social Media Roots Further into Daily Life during my Plunge into Deeper Adulthood

It was in Seattle when I first fired up an Instagram account. I was almost 30 years old at this point. I guess the Facebook platform had become less cool and the new hot place to post was on the photo-based app Instagram.

I posted nature pictures there. Photos of places I snowboarded and hiked in the Cascade mountains. I posted a picture of a die-cast Wizard figure with a magnifying glass set in the snow and a purple solar lens flare created by aiming my iphone's aperture into the sunlight. These posts had very little captions and I knew nothing of algorithms. I solely posted because I wanted to share what I was doing with the people who followed me through my community networks over the years.

Some writer resources had spoken about how writers should have a Twitter account so I fired one up. I posted a few things but living on the platform or meeting daily post quotas never appealed to me.

I dabbled with posting scrappy music videos of my guitar songs on YouTube, still knowing nothing of algorithms, attention-grabbing hooks, or clickbait titles. I solely wanted to create, hit publish, and move on to more creating.

Being out of the mountain incubator and in the big city now, I quickly realized the harsh truth about the real world. Life was expensive and getting more expensive. Making more money was a must. My Spanish skills landed me a bilingual insurance claims transcriptionist job, which then landed me a contract position at Amazon testing the kindle dictionaries in Spanish and French.

The contract was extended once and when it ran out a headhunting company placed me in a software testing job at a bank. The pay was better than I had ever had but the work was bland and methodical. There was no creative expression in it. The gulf between how it made me feel and how my creative endeavors made me feel was still vast. I could not easily transition between both sides of that gap. My creative striving was still a reflection of my broken romantic yearning.

***

In Seattle I attempted to make a pilot episode for a comedy series I wanted to produce that followed aspiring actors in the dating realm. I roped actors and a videographer into the project unpaid. I gave my dog Zeus a role as a bacon eating Rottweiler. We had a good team and the actors were funny but the good times didn't last for long. My personal life hit a wall mid-production.

I was unhappy with my software testing job and life in the city. On top of that Zeus at age ten became suddenly diagnosed with a life-threatening tumor, and a lover I'd been dating moved from Seattle to the very mountains of Colorado I had come here from. I hadn't been the best version of myself to her. I was still reeling from past romantic disappointments and my parents divorce and it affected my behavior and ability to be truly present and appreciate what we had. She left because she couldn't handle my fear of commitment and lack of self-love anymore.

One day when Zeus couldn't stand because the tumor had siphoned off too much of his blood, I took him to the vet. They suggested putting him down right then and there. I couldn't support that option.

The other option was to pay for a blood transfusion and get him on steroids and blood clotting medications. I couldn't stand to see him die in the city, far from the mountains that had been our home. I paid for the operation, called off work and drove Zeus back to Crested Butte the very next day. Crossing the deserts of our continent to get home, he sniffed at the plethora of smells across the West and barked at the passing Thunders.

***

We cut into the Central Mountains East of the Grand Mesa near the Black Canyon's downstream exit and up towards our old stomping grounds. Zeus had laid down most of the trip in pain, but when we arrived here and I opened the window, he stood and hung his head out, wagging his little nub of a tail. We had made it back home.

Here in the height of summer, I reconnected with the ex-lover and her dog and we took Zeus on his last adventures.

He got a whole week to explore his old stomping grounds. He rolled in snow, fetched big logs from the Slate River, and ate a dead fish. One day he couldn't stand again and I knew it was his time.

I took him to the vet. When she administered the shot, I was forehead to forehead with Zeus. As his heart beat its last beats, he reached his paw out to stay with me. The vet told me he was a fighter. I closed my eyes and saw visions of the mountain basin where I had lived and adopted Zeus.

The drive back to Seattle was tough. This loss of my best friend had broken me further. I felt like my dreams and the inevitable disappointments of life had gotten tangled.

I returned to the unfinished film project I had started. Most the actors wanted to continue the production, but one was asking for money and the videographer said he could no longer work unpaid. The fearless leader energy I'd carried into the production now felt weak and breakable, like I'd been punched in the gut and had gotten the wind knocked out of me and could no longer stand.

The vet in Colorado called and said they had Zeus ashes and asked for a shipping address. I told them to hold them and that I would move back and come get them in person.

I called the film production off and abandoned my hopes of becoming a famous filmmaker, musician, and writer in Seattle. My personal life was more important than that fantasy. I had clung too much to the way I hoped it would happen and not to the way it felt. I quit my job, packed up and decided to move back to the mountains and try to rekindle the romance with the lover who had left me.

On the return journey I drove the Highway 101 down the coast and filmed acoustic music performances in different locations along the way, all intended for YouTube. I filmed on the edge of steep and rugged Oregon coastal cliffs with the Pacific Ocean stretching beyond the horizon. I filmed amongst tall blades of grass blowing in the breeze in the Sand Dunes between Oregon and California. I performed a verbose and poetic song written for the long lost poetess lover amongst the tall Redwoods.

I wanted to continue the drive down the entire coastline of the lower 48 States, but my road turned East from San Francisco. I visited my Sister there for a night and then crossed the basin and range country of Nevada on the Loneliest Highway eastward. I filmed another song of mine upon a dried lake bed not far from where years later I filmed the content of my broken down car when I was stranded in the Desert of Nicheless Souls.

All of these went up on my YouTube and got under 50 views. I cared more about creating from what I felt inside and cared nothing for social media growth. After each post I moved on with my life.

My heart lead me back to the mountain town I had come here from. I moved in with the lover from Seattle who I had come back to the mountains for. We gave it a second go. We spread my dogs' ashes on mountains he and I had summited. I kept up Instagram nature posts when I felt like it and posted occasional YouTube music videos while I worked as a Performing Arts Manager at a haunted non-profit arts center that used to be a brothel in the 1800s.

The job entailed marketing our events locally. This was my first direct job duty that entailed marketing via social media posting. Before this I had been in snowboard instruction, hospitality, education, Spanish translation/interpretation, and software quality assurance. Now I put on art events. We used newspaper ads, radio spots, printed fliers, websites, and social media to promote them.

This primarily entailed Facebook posts on our Arts Center page but I took it a step further and made some YouTube video trailers for the Christmas play I directed and put on with a local cast of kids and adults. Over the course of 5 nights of performances, I set my camera up on a tripod and put together a full YouTube video of the play. It maybe got a few hundred views or less.

It was part of the job to post on social media. I did my duties to get a measly paycheck.

Though I had finally gotten paid in the arts, it wasn't a gainfully employed wage and so I began seeking other opportunities. On top of that, the romance did not work out for a second time and I decided my prospects were better back in a highly populated metropolis area. I took a job with a salary and benefits at the central office of Denver Public Schools.

Before I left the arts center I put on a singer songwriter showcase and performed as one of the acts with other local musicians. Facebook posts helped us fill the seats. It was an honor to perform on stage with other musicians.

When it was over, I packed up and headed away from the mountains of my heart to secure a salaried paycheck with benefits in the big city.

Chapter 3

Navigating Healing, a 9-5, and Creative Survival

The next job was bland and boring and required being in the office 8 hours a day with a button up shirt on except for fridays. It wasn't creative but it paid better than the Arts Center did.

They gave me a stand up desk. I remember looking out the 14th floor windows of the lounge at a sliver of the mountains through a gap between the city's buildings. Once upon a time before there was a city Buffalo had roamed here on vast rolling plains, tall grasses swaying in the breeze.

I felt cut off from an important part of myself. The wildness of the Landscapes I loved the most were now a several hours drive away. You could get to the mountains beside Denver, but they weren't the places I longed to explore most. Many weekends I drove four hours one way to be in the mountains I wanted to. I was here in the city for the job and to find my grounding again.

During this time I published my second novel Poet for Hire. It was already written and I had been sitting on it so I didn't have any extra creation to do. I made one Instagram post and called it good. I was embarrassed to have spent years of my life working on a novel that only reminded me about the poetess lover that it hadn't worked out with and who I should have let go of long ago.

I told friends I had carried the project on longer than I should have. I had left a wound open to source material from for far too long when it should have healed and I could have been better in my last relationship. I vowed "that I may not ever write another novel again."

I carried on and started a band with some friends. Part Time Ghost was our name. I made a couple music videos and we recorded an album during the covid pandemic.

At this point of my life I had been back in the city a few years and it was wearing on me. I preferred the rural lifestyle. I drove to the mountains every chance I got to snowboard or hike. It was my way of grounding myself in presence and joy. The trips often lasted just a weekend and then I was back to the city life.

The job dealt with educating teachers and principals about a testing software. It introduced me to the idea of a email newsletter and video tutorials. I wrote weekly newsletters for over 200+ schools and got some mailchimp practice. This provided some grounding in practical skills that were useful to others.

Though the practice and skills were useful and brought in financial resources, the subject matter was still not anything that nurtured my soul. I was writing about how to use software for school tests. I hated tests as a kid. The essay where I had to express opinion got me through grade school and college, not my multiple choice test scores. Because the

29

job was void of purposeful engagement for me, I sought relief in social media. I used it for distraction, not self improvement.

During this time my social media feed was hijacked by Only Fans models. My engagement habits exposed my male weakness for female beauty which the algorithm exploited ruthlessly. The longer I was on the platform staring into the digital pixel blaze of female flesh, the more time they had to hit me with ads.

I doom-scrolled my Instagram feed. The swipe to the next content more often than not revealed a new expression of external female beauty in its prime. On social media, the models didn't need a deep intellectual thought or a thought provoking verbal hook to seize attention. Their hooks were to expose 75-90% of their flesh, jiggle back and forth, and put it to music. It worked very well on me. They earned my attention with free follows but never got me to click through to their exclusive realms. I knew I wanted a real connection not a digital library.

I followed models, and then the algorithm fed me more of their model friends. Soon I was following hundreds of them. I'd swipe through my feed getting cheap dopamine hit after cheap dopamine hit. I took this cheap dopamine addiction further by constantly swiping through the options on what I call digital mating apps.

I was exposed to dating apps (mating apps) in Seattle and I knew it brought the promise of quick connections. Instead of working on my own healing and my creative projects after publishing my second book, I sought connection and fornication on the digital mating apps.

Peacocks and grouse strut their beautiful feathers to mate while humans post their best pictures and swipe digital representations of flesh. We type descriptions in our profile that we think will be most appealing to the right kind of partner. For me, I was scared being myself would alienate myself from a shot at being loved, so I tried to make my profile as broadly appealing as possible.

Friends who used the mating apps too discussed ways of trying to keep it cool and casual and not scare off potential mating partners. Pictures always were a mix of yourself in different environments: casual but cool, dressed up, doing an outdoor activity.

I cycled through all kinds of photos of myself: me on a mountain, me dressed up at a wedding, me holding my guitar. We posted whatever we could to give the appearance of being unique, when instead we could have simply lived that way and attracted the right mates through our natural gravity of being. We were impatient though and could not wait on destiny.

When used as an escape, social media and dating apps became a distraction from the greater purpose of self improvement and expression. I made the music with the band and that was a great experience, though how much more could I have grown if I had spent time on self-improvement habits and continued my prose writing or filmmaking or even put in extra effort with the music?

***

After three years of the office job, I was bored. The cost of life and my extreme appetite for experiences still had me wanting more money. I needed a new environment and set of responsibilities. I began looking for new jobs. A friend of a friend hired me through an informal hiring process to make videos and write marketing copy for his YouTube ads software and coaching business as well as two of his Youtube channels.

The company's YouTube channel on running YouTube ads we started from scratch and his personal YouTube channel was about growing Marijuana. I shot and edited videos for both brands. We filmed marijuana growing tutorial videos where I zoomed in on aphid insects and the crystals of the buds in his garage. I filmed YouTube ad business videos in his office where he spoke about ads and did screen recording setup demos on his computer. The in-person shooting was only required every couple weeks.

My job went primarily remote, and I went harder on my road trips for mountain explorations than ever before. I drove to Crested Butte, the San Juan Mountains, Utah, Jackson Hole, Montana, and even managed two trips deep into Canada during winter for snowboarding. I was gone often and missed band practice a lot. That travel lust got me kicked out of the band. I wasn't around enough to stay tight on our songs.

When they said they wanted to do Part Time Ghost without me, it hit me harder than I admitted to myself. To mask the disappointment, I turned it into a joke: "There's always one guy in a rock band with a powder addiction that affects their commitment." The powder of course wasn't cocaine, but the kind that falls from the sky. The joke was that I was addicted to snowboarding like many rock stars were addicted to cocaine or other substances.

After I got kicked out of the band there was less desire for creativity. The disappointments of perceived failure after perceived failure in the arts made me want to only engage in activities that I knew always felt good.

My form of self expression became walking routes through the mountains or snowboarding powder-draped faces. It was about standing in remote places at the pinnacles of upthrust land. Most the time I was solo. Few friends had the time and location freedom I had nor the compulsion and dedication to drive as far as I did. More than anything, I craved the solitude and the alone time. It's hard to get disappointed if you only rely on yourself for joy.

I told myself creative expression wasn't for me. That I couldn't balance a job, outdoor passions, and soul work. I still desired though.

I still desired though. I tracked everything. I made long lists categorized by life subject. There was a list for mountain peaks to summit, screenplays and books and songs to write, exercise routines to do, places to travel. I called this growing list my Cosmic To-Do List. It was everything I felt I had to do in this life before I died.

Yet the truth was that I couldn't do all these things at once. I felt I had to pick. Since my creative pursuits carried the scars of perceived failure, I chose the mountains. They were my medicine. They were always there for me standing tall and bold, conjurers of weather and wonder.

***

I don't consider work projects as art. Business projects have an aim of delivering tangible value to someone else in exchange for resources (aka money). Business projects therefore evaluate the perceived value before releasing it to the world. I see art or creative expression as something you create because your soul must create it. It is expression without being pre-filtered through the lens of perceived value and a potential return on investment.

I told myself it was too difficult to prioritize creative self-expression in our hustle-focused economy. I felt I was not able to fully and completely pursue my natural interests and passions to their highest level because of work's time and energy commitment. I complained it drained the stamina of my creative focus.

Instead of finding solutions to create, I attached my identity to what I did for work. I suddenly felt proud to tell people I worked in marketing. I thought I'd be more appealing in the dating pool because of my job title and new career field.

I see this often in our times where we over-identify with what we do for work. We may feel deep down there's something more we're supposed to be doing, something truer, something that's uniquely ours, but work swallows up so much time and mental bandwidth that we just attach our personal identity and uniqueness to our job.

Then there are all the other responsibilities:

To our bodies, if we choose to care for them with exercise and healthy diet.

To play and recreation which is essential but can sometimes become just another form of escape.

To other people — partners, kids, loved ones who need us.

All of it becomes part of the story we use to define ourselves. Sometimes we cling to those identities so hard that we lose track of who we actually are beneath the labels.

I remember telling people I was "in marketing," that I was a "Director of Content," like it was some badge of honor. Like finally having a decent job meant I was winning at life.

I felt that becoming good at repressing my natural calling and engaging in the work that paid bills and provided a surplus of resources was the way to be respected and rewarded.

Yet the truth was I was hiding behind that job title. While I was busy saying that's who I was and I should be validated for, I wasn't:

Writing.

Creating music.

Working on creative projects that felt real to me.

I wasn't using the skills and natural forms of expression that felt true.

Instead, I used the job title as a shield, a way to avoid the vulnerability of admitting I wasn't living the creative life I wanted.

I think a lot of us do that in today's world. We hide behind our titles, our resumes, our LinkedIn headlines when deep down, we know those labels aren't the whole story nor the actual goal.

There's nothing wrong with being proud of what you do. I guess I was jealous of people who were proud of their job and I was judgemental of people who made their job their whole sense of self worth. Some people get enough fulfillment from their job and their daily goals and there is nothing wrong there. It just has never worked out for me for long. There was always something else I wanted to be working on, and I could never quite make the time nor muster the courage to do it at the level of intensity I craved.

Though I did shoot and edit YouTube videos, ads, video sales letters, and write marketing emails at my new job, I was still not creating from my own self expression. I was promoting someone else's messaging. I was writing in the brand voice, not my own.

We also did weekly affiliate email promotions. Often we would get an offer with pre-written marketing emails that we'd rewrite in the CEO's voice. They were all for digital products I had never used or ever heard of, yet I promoted them by means of false scarcity. Our target audience was people who suffered from a bad case of FOMO. They feared missing out on some hack to make more money.

The intention of the writing and videos I produced were to sell software, courses, and coaching programs that helped online advertisers. I was manufacturing content. Not storytelling from my own personal lore.

I managed a content calendar where we published one YouTube video a week, converted it into a written blog post on our website, and emailed our list several times per week. A hired company covered the LinkedIn posts under the CEO's name. The posts were nothing he wrote or felt empowered to share as his personal mission. The company handled the posts and a community of people in their network commented on them to boost engagement.

Between video shoots & edits, email marketing, and content calendar management, the CEO and I would meet in his office. He would cue up a pre-recorded automated webinar that we had just filled from ads and the email list. He opened a bottle of mezcal with a bell on top and we toasted morning shots as we watched the sales come in from the webinar.

This was the new revolutionary business model of the 21st century. Promise them a secret solution to a pain point they have. Agitate that pain point. Then introduce the solution and the offer and ignite a fear of tackling this problem without your offer as their ally. This was digital piracy in its sleekest form. We felt like we had cracked the code to freedom. But some part of me knew that this wasn't art nor expression. This was a performance of freedom, not the real thing.

This job felt like working on a pirate ship for a Captain who refused to accept the norms of business. He narrated our business videos in shorts and a t-shirt, his long curly hair grown beyond his shoulders. He would wear t-shirts for the band Tool or a tye-dye shirt that said "Legalize Acid." We made sales from this content. The company got up to over a million a year.

I saw how my friend who owned the company had so much free time and could cancel a company meeting when he was on a trip. Other than being in person once a month or so to shoot videos, I could work from anywhere. I embraced road life and learned how to be efficient at my job while on workcation. I could snowboard whenever it snowed.

I was now fully immersed in the online marketing world and was learning about small business operations online. I could pursue my outdoor hobbies as hard as I wanted within the confines of a flexible monday through friday work schedule, and could get paid doing it.

I had my survival and recreational needs covered. Life was comfortable and convenient. Who needed to express their soul's inner story when it was all too painful and difficult to sustain anyway?

Chapter 4

Over-Identifying with Work to Hide from Truth

"Alright, action," I said as I pushed record on the camera.

My employer took a deep breath to get into his advertisement persona. We were in his office with his own set decorated to his personality. Two green fabric chairs were against a wooden wall with a poster from the band Tool framed on the wall and a couple skulls of animals he collected.

He began speaking to the camera.

"Want to learn my super secret magic trick on how to turn one dollar into 8 dollars using simple YouTube ads just like this one?"

He rattled off an improvised ad without having a script. He had used these phrases for years. I sat behind the camera, monitoring the audio levels and taking notes on my phone in our project management software of things he said that needed to be included in the final production of the ad.

When he had effectively narrated the problem, pain points, the solution, his own unique method, and a call to action he stopped talking.

"That's probably good," he said.

I stopped recording.

We had shot about 5 ad angles, a video sales letter, and a couple organic YouTube videos for the business in a couple hour shoot.

"I'll go transfer the footage and get started editing," I said.

I left the office and went to my desk out in the main co-working space. As I transferred the footage to my external hard drive the company's media buyer sent me a message with a link on our communication platform Slack.

"Good ad copy to study for our stuff," he wrote.

I clicked the link.

It took me to a page with the headline "3 Secrets to Reach 1000 YouTube Subscribers and get Monetized in 3 Months."

I had seen lots of outrageous claims about ways to make money online in this job. We ran many affiliate marketing campaigns via email promoting other people's offers. If we made a sale to our email list, we would receive a commission for it. Many of the titles offered various methods on how to monetize digital assets and make money.

This one my coworker had sent spoke to me. I was already managing our company YouTube channel and sitting back while our CEO did all the talking to the camera.

Why couldn't I also do the same thing for myself?

That way I could have even more time to roadtrip, snowboard in the winter, backpack in the summer, and travel across the land without having to be back to set up the camera, lights, microphones, push record and then spend hours editing.

I scanned the sales page and watched the video sales letter. It pitched a short mini-course on starting a YouTube channel and using it to promote an offer or service. I was all in. I purchased it, sent myself the link to get started after work, and then got to editing our company videos we had just shot.

When the work day wrapped up, I got in my car and drove back down to the city from the Front Range mountains. The commute wasn't bad but it wasn't ideal. I could work from anywhere for weeks at a time before having to be in person. I got home and instead of engaging in any of my own projects, I opened the new course I had bought and started studying.

At this time, my YouTube, Instagram and email inbox feeds were getting pummeled with ads and offers about different ways to accomplish the same thing: make more money online while working less. Everyone had their own method. Everyone claimed their method was the only right way to do it. Every other way was wrong. If I didn't take action now I would miss out.

This method of self-promotion created reliance on a constant feed of new information. It bred information addiction and prohibited unhindered experimentation. Many of these personal brands seemed to capitalize on people's fears of imperfection and their fear of missing out. I always felt I had to buy one more course or watch five more YouTube videos before I could really get started.

This led to me purchasing more courses than I had time to study, and kept me consuming more and more content without taking action. I was studying get rich quick schemes that perpetuated inaction. They weren't all spammy courses but even the legit ones fed the same addiction and distanced me from my more natural calling.

There were niches for everything: filmmaking, ecommerce, affiliate marketing, consulting, email marketing, pinterest mastery, how to become a personal brand influencer-- niches on niches on niches. It was like there were niches on how to make 12 million dollars in sales on autopilot while soaking in your mountain hot tub.

There was always something more to study and understand before I could get started and put together my own offer.

I had always had ADHD and always felt I had to investigate every possible option before taking action. I traveled down content wormholes. Click a link and open in a new tab, and then go back to the original search tab to open a fuck ton more tabs to study later before you go study the one you had clicked on in the first place.

The information age and social media had brought instant knowledge and new skills to our fingertips at nearly the speed of light. Yet the downside was information overload and decision fatigue resulting in an inability to make decisions and take action.

Over the coming months I studied online entrepreneurship methods as my creative side withered away. To deal with the pain of repressing my heart's calling to express myself, I went snowboarding or hiking and went on dates from the digital mating apps. I drove back and forth between the city, the mountain coworking office, and the deeper mountains.

***

Between trips, I managed to get one little creative project off the ground.

Being disenchanted with all this content creator education, a friend and I started co-writing YouTube episode scripts for a satirical comedy series that made fun of the idea of "getting rich on YouTube." The show was called "How to Get Rich on YouTube." We discussed the idea of each playing satirical versions of ourselves as the two main characters. This was a side project that was my creative outlet when I had stopped playing guitar and writing books.

At one point my employer suggested I start my own business. He said "you should just start your own LLC and I'll pay you."

This further tickled my desire for freedom and to be my own boss. The idea of being able to set my own schedule and call off from work whenever I wanted and for however long I wanted like he did was highly appealing. My employer called off our weekly sync meetings on Mondays when he was on vacation with his family or had concerts to go to.

Why couldn't I do the same with my adventures and ranging the land?

The truth was I practically already had that time freedom. The concept of giving employees flexible time off and work schedules had already taken root in our culture, showing that employees were happier and thus more productive. Some may argue against this but the idea had been embraced by a lot of companies. My boss was no exception and he allowed us to take time off for personal reasons. As long as our work got done he didn't mind and we still got paid. This was a healthy work environment and the biggest sense of freedom I had ever had in a job. I still wanted more. As the hunger for more travel and adventure intensified, so did my big spender habit.

The CEO of the company and I called off work and went on hunting trips in the fall. When I was working though, he was always hitting me up on the private DMs on the company slack to send me new hunting gear recommendations or suggesting various crypto currencies and NFTs to buy.

He made more than me owning the company so these purchases may not have been a big deal to him. To me every suggestion that interrupted my work for the company became more temptations and influences to spend. There was always something I wanted to buy so I bought more and more things. These purchases led to the acquisition of ever more recreational gear on top of my collection of digital courses and memberships.

With my addictions to recreation, I couldn't save for the life of me and the company offered no retirement account. The desire to make more and more continued. I was like a Hungry Hungry Hippo. Due to all the freedom I had at my friend's company, I remained loyal and didn't apply for better paying jobs. I thought the only way to make unlimited income and have unlimited time freedom was to make it working for myself.

I had the desire to work for myself but lacked the conviction to declare a niche and follow through and set up an offer. I kept studying digital marketing methods and online business models like the ruthless acquisition of knowledge proved something.

I studied YouTube, Instagram, email marketing, and other audience building methodologies. Likes and subscribers and view counts were all the rage. There was no talk about the mission behind the content. Nothing about following your intuition. It was all virality and numbers flex.

I became enamored with the concept of working less while earning more through the act of content creation. It seemed like a new revolutionary work model. I over-identified with the act and fantasy of its success instead of identifying with a mission statement rooted in my own personal experience.

I fell for the promise of it. It seemed like a solution to an eternal conflict that existed in my life even before this supposed work revolution.

For well over a decade now I had struggled with the idea of how I could live a life where work consumed less of my creative force, had less hold over my time and schedule, and took up less of my emotional bandwidth. I had been in pursuit of learning how we can survive and thrive in comfort while living in alignment with our purpose. It had always been hard for me to pursue extra personal goals outside of work. Yet that is also based on the choices we make and how we manage our time.

I remember my Dad telling me we had to have a means of supporting ourselves and that we can't do everything we want in life. He was just speaking from a place of experience and personal pain from that hard truth. Yet to me it came with a berating tone. He wanted me to succeed and thought my writing ideas were cool, he had been a big reader as a young man himself, but he had chosen the safe secure career path to provide for a family of 5.

Sensitive me took it all to heart. He delivered the hard truth but offered no consolation nor solution on how to do the things that mattered most. Perhaps he didn't know the answer. That was on me to figure out.

The content creator promise of financial and time abundance was an outlet for the pain I carried. It wasn't about influence or clout, but about reclaiming life itself. I carried a bitter rage and frustration at the way things had transpired in my life. I loved creative expression and the great outdoors but felt torn between them. I was angry at the extra lift required to do my soul's work outside of a 9-5, and still also take care of myself emotionally and physically.

Yet even in ancient times before 9-5s existed, you had to work hard to survive. Hunting, farming, building, and grinding bread. To create art after all that was extra work. In essence the hard truth has always been the same.

Now though, I had a promised solution. The content creator economy beckoned with new hope. Long before I ever shot a Reel, I'd felt the tension between work and living. I wanted to play music, write, snowboard, and wander the mountains but there was never enough time to do it all to the level of depth and intensity I craved.

The content creator dream seemed like a revolution: a way to work less, earn more, and finally live more fully. It felt like the only modern path to freedom.

If I could just make a profitable business that ran on one-person business, I could have all the time I'd need to explore the mountains AND create to my heart's content.

***

At this point I had lived in the big city of Denver for 5 years. I was burned out from all the driving I did to get to the places I wanted to explore only to turn around after an adventure and drive hours and hours back to the city.

I had been unhappy in the city. My soul felt displaced. I longed to live closer to the areas I had been driving hours to see. I asked my employer if he'd mind if I moved to my favorite mountain range in Southwest Colorado. The one I felt called to explore the most. I promised I'd still drive up to record our videos.

He answered as a friend and not a boss.

"Yea I don't care, dude," he said.

With that approval, I arranged the move to the remote mountains in the other corner of Colorado. I had become such a slave to employment that I had to consult someone else before making a life decision for myself.

The stage was set to make a change. I arranged the move. Housing was difficult to find in the autumn of that year in Southwest Colorado. Housing shortages were already a problem in Colorado mountain towns and most leases had been signed at summer's end for the winter.

I managed to find a one bedroom apartment in a converted hotel at the base of Purgatory Ski Resort. The terrain wasn't as gnarly as I'd like for a ski resort but it was in the San Juan mountains where I wanted to be. I could walk to the ski lift and get a few runs in before or during work. The Weminuche Wilderness was right across the street. Access to many mountains was only a very short drive away. The small city of Durango was a half hour away. I could grocery shop and get a fix of socializing and still get to the deep mountains.

I told my friend I had been co-writing the YouTube scripts with that I was moving and the production of our episodes would be strained. He was more immersed in his own prose writing and didn't mind. He had been engaged in the script writing as a creative exercise not as something he hoped to produce.

I packed up a U-haul and moved my belongings across the mountains to the other side of the state. I brought my ambitions for financial and time freedom with me, along with all the various ideas and methods for attaining it. I also brought the seed of the concept for the episodic comedy series "How to Get Rich on YouTube."

I thought having the vast wilderness as my neighbor and less population density would help me focus and find the courage to start. It was bound to happen and would only be a matter of time before I was living larger than I ever had before.

This was the age of the creator economy where you could live life on your own terms.

Act II

The Living Creator Experiment:

In Pursuit of the Soul Niche

Chapter 5

Content Creation in the Deep Mountains

Google's AI Overview describes a niche for online business as " a specific, focused segment of a larger market where a company chooses to specialize, allowing them to cater to a particular set of customers with unique needs and interests, differentiating themselves from broader competitors within that market."

The Oxford Dictionary has several definitions for the word niche.
/niCH,nēSH/

noun

1.
   a comfortable or suitable position in life or employment.
   "he is now a partner at a leading law firm and feels he has found his niche"
2.
   a specialized segment of the market for a particular kind of product or service.
   "he believes he has found a niche in the market"

adjective

> denoting products, services, or interests that appeal to a small, specialized section of the population.
> "other companies in this space had to adapt to being niche players"

verb

> place (something) in a niche or recess
> "these elements were niched within the shadowy reaches"

Many of the online business gurus used the phrase "to niche down" as a verb when describing how to categorize your content area expertise. The act of niching down was designed to isolate a single problem that a certain group of people have that you focus your business offering or content focus on.

My problem was that deep down I knew finding a profitable business niche would not fulfill what my spirit longed for. My mind couldn't grasp this truth though. I thought the discovery of my profitable niche would free me.

Deep down, I longed for a shift in my belief that I didn't have time to make the art projects I wanted to. After experiencing what I perceived as my creative failures, I retreated into disdain that working made me creatively inefficient. I didn't want resource acquisition to drain all my energy during my peak focus hours. I also wanted to be able to explore the land widely and still have time to be creative without it being hard on my bank account or inconvenience my schedule and daily routines.

Deep down I knew money would be nice. Yet I also knew it wouldn't solve the truth that I longed to get back to my fervor for creating writing, music, and narrative videos from a place of expression, wonder, and curiosity. Not from a place of trying to harvest money from others as the primary goal. Having the profitable business wouldn't be the thing that changed my creative mindset and commitment to creative ritual. Yet I believed I had to create content that earned partially passive income to then take control of my schedule, not worry about money, and express in the arts to my heart's content.

The truth was I wanted to be known for my storytelling and expression, not for a business specialty. I wanted to engage all my interests, passions, and skillsets into a single endeavor or brand that encompassed the full expanse of my spirit. I was reluctant to fully commit to a full business model because I feared that declaring one single business niche would jeopardize the truth I was seeking for my soul.

What part of me would have died if I committed fully to the path of content for profitability and owned it as my creative identity?

***

At first living in the mountains was all excitement and making new friends. I continued working the job remotely and once a month or so drove six hours one way across the many mountain ranges of Colorado to the coworking office in the Northern Mountains to shoot video.

When at home, I explored the new terrain at Purgatory ski resort. It wasn't very steep or extreme but I cruised the woods and found small cliffs to jump off when the snow was deep. Beyond the new home resort, my powder chasing addiction was still in full swing. I owned 4 ski passes and since I was primarily a remote worker, I monitored the OpenSnow app's snow forecasts constantly. I was always ready at a day's notice to drive to distant mountain ranges if they were getting more snow than my home resort.

I documented my travels and excitement on Instagram stories. I posted screenshots of the snow forecast totals, screenshots of my google map driving routes, and pictures of myself with a snowbeard and handheld videos of me snowboarding steep lines.

In the midst of the blizzards I drove 6+ hours for, I received email notifications from the content gurus for limited time offers. They even came in while I was riding the slopes. Their attempts at direct response marketing failed to work on me when I was in my element, snowboarding steeps while the blizzard howled and delivered fresh refills.

As I lived out my powder chasing dreams, I was told by internet personalities on social media that I should be posting. They said my niche should be based on my interests. I thought back to all my interests over the years. I had wanted to be an actor. A writer. A filmmaker. A musician. I felt like jobs and my need for exploring the mountains kept me from staying with one thing long enough for it to grow into any semblance of foundation and abundance.

I spent hours and emotions ruminating on what the ideal niche for me was. What was truest to my natural, most authentic self? I had been an explorer of self expression. I liked telling stories and the sudden winds of curiosity. If I was to create content for social media I needed to incorporate all of these themes.

Yet the gurus in all the courses I had bought and the content I saw online said you had to deliver value to people. To be profitable, you had to create something that others wanted. Since my interests were vast and many, I decided content creation as a niche was broad enough to incorporate many themes.

I declared content creator as my new niche. I surrendered to it as my creative identity.

In truth EVERYTHING in existence is content. Everything is the contents of the cosmos. Any new idea, object, meal, or work of art is the creation of content. Yet to do it in this day and age is to digitize ideas, concepts, or frameworks for consumption online. Becoming a content creator hadn't really narrowed my niche down. What was true was that I was committing to posting SOMETHING regularly online. This is what the content creator role of the times demanded.

Declaring myself a content creator meant that I would share images, thoughts, ideas, quotes, places, and my speaking publicly and often. This was a change from taking years to write a novel in seclusion and then only half-heartedly sharing it because I had already moved on inside from the themes.

A niche that was my very own existed within the broader niche of content creation. I wanted to act satire about content creators and the hyper-enthusiastic and flawed individual trying to share their message online. I wanted to make content about myself as a content creator figuring out what to make content about. It was satire mockumentary disguised as documentary. THAT was my content.

***

I've always been a bit of a method actor in my own life. To understand something, I have to live it. When I set out to become a content creator, I didn't just study it. I became the living experiment.

I wanted to method act it and present it in a way where I seemed like I was deadly serious about the content even though I was creating fictional narratives. Deep down in my soul, I knew that I thought being a content creator / personal brand advice guy was untrue to myself. It was a manufacturer of content, a regurgitator of processes, an algorithm hacker. It was not an expressor of feeling. Yet I was called to storytelling and it was through this commitment to play the content creator guru role as a flawed individual that I would weave my stories.

When I told myself I gave up creativity, it was as a living example to show people how repressing your inner natural calling is not the way to happiness and fulfillment. It was my weird form of rebellion against society's newest work role. I did it by showing the mess that happens when you forsake your truth to follow the herd and conform to trends. The truth was no one cared to fix that mess. Everyone had their own messes themselves to work on. If anyone was going to fix my own mess it had to be myself.

This habit had roots that stretched deep into my childhood immaturity. I often played the living example even when it wasn't good for me.

At age 4 or so my Dad stopped reading me my storybook to answer a phone call. I wanted to show how upset I was that he interrupted story time so I stormed down the basement steps and accidentally stumbled, rolled, and broke my arm. I paid the price of trying to be a living example of why it's not good to interrupt storytime.

Later in my twenties, I had a tendency to become the living experiment.

My old childhood friend once told me I didn't party enough anymore. This was after I had gotten over the brunt of my raging party-addict habit. I wanted to make him happy though as well as show the severity of his wishes.

So one night back home visiting in Milwaukee, Wisconsin I tried to 'play the part.' I drank a lot of booze like my younger self had. When he drove me home after the party, I had to piss so he pulled over on a back road by the lake. I got out to pee but could barely stand straight. He had to hold me up by the shirt collar so I wouldn't fall face-first into my own stream of piss.

The lengths I went to to live an experience or prove a point were extreme. I wanted to show my friend that the sloppy drunk version of me wasn't the best version of myself. I was a man of extremes.

It was like I was always performing for the social situations I found myself in, even when the script didn't fit me. Often, the role was a way to hide from my real questions — about who I was, and what I wanted to create.

Deep down, I didn't want to make content about a profitable niche like marketing or personal brand tactics. I wanted to reforge my union with my inner artist and embrace his innocence. I wanted to forgive his naivety at thinking art would be easy and that monetary compensation would be a natural side effect of my expression.

I wanted to remind my inner artist that being your authentic self and letting your creations manifest naturally was simple when you don't force it and you are not attached to outcome. When you're not trying to prove anything to anyone about who you are.

In truth, the creations arrive naturally when you are in alignment with your soul purpose. I wanted to remind myself this, but I was going to take the long road to do so. I was going to have to feel and experience everything along the way.

I invented a series for social media. Video reels were the new art form. I based the premise on the "How to Get Rich on YouTube" scripts my friend and I wrote about the YouTube influencers. I wanted to play the role of someone who was trying to build an audience on social media. Someone who claims to know how to hack the algorithm to make enough money to quit your 9 to 5 job but in truth was just mimicking the posting habits of other content creators and unknowingly bringing their own authentic personality to the content.

The character was Brady C Snow. At times I posted from my natural passions and travels. Other times I was performing as myself in the role of flawed content creator.

It was easier and cheaper than making a feature film. I assumed my business offer would eventually be about building an audience. Deep down, that was not what I wanted to offer. All I really wanted was to create and experiment and release to the world and move on and continue creating.

My mind and heart diverged. My mind went down the path of hope for followers while my heart followed the path of expressing what was natural to me even if it was satire.

***

I started production. I called the series "Whats my Nitch?" The episodes were numbered. They started at negative numbers with decimal points and counted upwards towards episode 0. My joke to myself was that I'd find my niche by episode 0.

I told myself this was for my business. I converted my personal Instagram account to a business account.

The offer: watch me express myself. I will perform for you. Oh my dear internet spectators, please validate my fragile self worth by upping my views count and giving me a like. I will make some of you laugh and show you how absurd social media performance can be.

Most would not get the content. I would have done my job.

I embraced the madman within. I had no choice but to love him.

The pilot episode featured me filling up water at a spring. I played a second character who looked exactly like me but in different clothes.

I walked up to myself filling water at a pipe and questioned the purity of the water and the character of the guy who fills water jugs out of rusty metal pipes. I performed my impression of an Elk call. It was a deranged wheezing whine. I stated a fact about the early ancestors of the Elk having had 6 inch tusks. Some people commented and thought it was funny. Others told me how weird I was.

Rick Rubin in his book The Creative Act said ""If you've truly created an innovative work, it's likely to alienate as many people as it attracts. The best art divides the audience. If everyone likes it, you probably haven't gone far enough." (201).

Success. I had divided it, but I'm not so sure everyone would call my bizarre reel "art." It didn't matter. I was on a trajectory now.

Back visiting family in Denver, I made an episode from my nieces' playground in my brother's backyard. In my mind it was a sailing ship.

I looked out at the horizon. I cut to a clip I had shot of the setting sun and clouds reflecting on the Great Salt Lake of Utah so it looked like I was on a sailing ship upon some mysterious oceanic realm.

I cut back to me on the playground.

"No niches out there."

My alter ego climbs up the kids' slide.

"You should try the treasure hunting niche!"

"Genius," I say as my alter ego slides away down the slide.
I move to the plastic mock-telescope mounted on the playground and aim it out into the distance. I look through it.

The video zooms into a shot of me with a big beard in a hot spring in the mountains looking back at this hopeful version of myself through binoculars.

I meant it to be a truer version of me who has embraced a more soulful niche.

"Treasure hunting," the present me says. "It's genius!"

I leap down the slide of the playground as if its the portal to the next scene, which it is.

I leap up from the slide, my brother's dog Moose follows me, and then I cut to myself at an abandoned mine in the San Juan Mountains.

I wear my Grandpa's Strike King bowling sunglasses from the 1970s. They have croakies and side panels. My hair is slicked back. I speak in a British accent.

I play the role of a treasure hunter on his social media account and narrate made up histories about the fictional Collapsing Jack Mine.

I was seeking the ghost of Ole Jimmy Crooked Spine, a miner who had died in the collapse of the mine. I improvised it all. I rolled with this continued story on subsequent episodes as the british treasure hunter version of me.

I paddleboarded on mountain lakes as the British treasure hunter and shot episodes out there during approaching thunderstorms.

"Land ho!" I shouted as I pulled to shore as thunder echoed in the background.

I shot an episode where the treasure hunter narrated an ad for a wizard stick. My set was on a San Juan mountain.

I shot an extreme paddleboarding episode.

I filmed an episode in a hot spring. Then it was time to switch the niche. I came clean and admitted I wasn't actually British.

I think I wanted to portray this character because as a teenager I had loved British accents. I had been drawn to the Poetess Lover the first night we met because we were both drunkenly speaking in British accents to each other. The gurus also said content creation was a path to riches, so I played into that as a joke.

I chose to be a treasure hunter in the San Juan mountains because riches had been sought here in the mines and the range carried legends lost to common knowledge. The series needed to be dynamic and change course often. This was how I could be true to my spirit of curiosity and exploration.

The non-fictional me playing the fictional version of myself embraced a new niche for the series. I became a social media content creator. I was back to the original theme of the series and my whole life dilemma at the time. I played myself looking for my niche in Las Vegas. My employer flew the team and I there for a work conference. We walked around the strip and the casinos at night and I shot episodes there.

I called Vegas the Niche Factory USA. I showed the casinos. At a Craps table sign I said "Oh crap, I crapped my pants." I filmed content from the drainage ditches of Vegas to the casinos.

A brass Eagle in a shop window inside the Venetian told me I should start a YouTube channel. I had my old YouTube channel with my music on it but had forgotten the password and couldn't access it. I would start a new channel dedicated to the idea of being a content creator. That was the new narrative direction the series would take when I returned back to Colorado. I would actually start a YouTube channel in real life to go along with this new narrative.

***

Outside of the episodes, real life continued to yield experiences. Back in Colorado from Vegas my employer and I went hunting under Rocky Mountain National Park by Grand Lake. I killed my second Elk with a single shot from my new Rifle. It was about a 220 yard shot. I shot from prone position downhill and gutted the Elk solo.

I hacked her apart and pulled her guts out and then broke down crying. I laid and cuddled with her head and thanked her for her life and wished her soul well on the next journey. I did not make a satirical episode about the kill but I took a selfie with the dead Elk's face and posted it as a disappearing story.

My close friend said the emotion I was trying to convey was a difficult one to express on social media. He may have been right. I didn't overanalyze. I felt what I felt and acted on it. I had posted the death of this brave Elk and my love for her even though I had been her killer.

My employer's younger brother and his friends helped me quarter the Elk. I carried her head to the top of a hill and set her down facing the direction her herd and her had been running when she dropped from my bullet. I wanted her soul to have a final resting place with a connection to the Land she had inhabited and raised her kin upon. I told her I wish her kin live their best lives and go on to breed many more Elk who come to know the sacredness of this Land.

I transported the Elk quarters back to the San Juans and got them processed. I now had natural Colorado grown meat to nourish me through the next episodes of *Whats My Nitch*, which had become part of a larger story—the story of me, the protagonist inside the personal brand experiment.

I had committed to this. I was in too deep to stop now.

***

Back in the day my storytelling and music offerings were born from life experience. They were devotions to spirit. I lived therefore I felt. I had to make sense of it. I hungered for meaning. I longed to be witnessed. I wore my heart on my sleeve. I was a writer in his own garden tending his fragile plants and herbs.

I had notebooks and click pens with padded grips. I had messy handwriting but it was my sacred chickenscrawl. I had word docs saved to my computer hard drive and not the cloud. I backed the docs up after every writing session on a thumb drive. I had my descriptions of the interplay between light and cloud. I had my metaphors for mountain shapes and the ways Weather moved over Landscapes.

My content creations were born from a promise. That you could abandon your dutiful post at the cubicle from 9-5 on Mondays through Fridays. That your voice packaged and posted could set you free.

The gurus carried algorithms, acronyms, and affiliate links. They had their unique selling propositions and their ideal customer profiles. They offered free download templates of the best performing social media hooks. Proven to retain attention and promised to grow your account. You would sound like everyone else but you would be making $10k per month and be well on your way to scaling past $100k per month.

Their message was simple: automate your offer. Monetize your niche. Get paid while you sleep. The digital offer had low delivery costs and thus high margins. They didn't completely lie. But they didn't tell the whole story either.

Many of them leveraged false scarcity. Discount timers ticking away before the price went up and the opportunity would be gone forever. They were masters of getting people to act on their fears.

Their ideal customer profile was people with low self esteem and who suffered from a fear of missing out. I acted on my desire to control my time, my thirst to fund unhindered creative rituals, and to break free of limitations on my passions. Yet what I was being trained to do was turn soulborn impulse into sales copy.

I studied the gurus' content like sacred texts. Brendan Burchard, Gary Vaynerchuck, Frank Kern and many others whose names and marketing emails infiltrated my inbox. Each one a prophet of scalable selfhood. They entered as praised authorities into my inbox but their voices are archived in no place of inspiration in my soul.

I wanted their methodologies to unlock my highest calling. Instead they led me further from it.

These were the ones who taught freedom through formulas. They were no charlatans. They didn't completely lie but they left out the true cost. They sold a version of the creator dream: scaled, systemized, stripped of soul. I bought the courses and I didn't finish them because they were boring. I studied the blueprints and then cast them aside. I told myself I was being strategic. That it would all work out.

What I didn't realize was that I wasn't trying to build a business. I was trying to build a mythology. I wasn't chasing monetization like the gurus advised. I was chasing my soul through a dead forest stripped of its foliage. Every branch bare. No leaves in sight.

***

I launched longer episodes on the new YouTube channel based on the theme of the "How to Get Rich on YouTube" scripts my friend and I had written. I cast a shadow of self-aware satire over myself because deep down, I knew it was absurd to repress my natural expression until I could afford my freedom. I was now an aspiring YouTuber acting as a YouTube expert. I played a fictitious version of myself that came across to others as the real me.

I played that version of myself—a content creator making content about making content—because deep down I didn't yet feel free enough to make the content my heart actually wanted to.

This was when I introduced Billy the Camera Guy who I also played on camera. He dressed like a hipster with thick-framed glasses and a backwards newsboy cap. He came across as more composed and grounded than Brady. He was the strategic and practical side of myself that my shoot-emotion-from-the-hip artist self never was.

Billy was the voice of reason and the subtle director and producer to Brady's madness and indecision. Together Brady and Billy started a YouTube channel with Brady Snow as the star of the show.

I filmed the act of Brady and Billy chasing the dream of making Brady a successful creator but I framed it as a satire of itself. A self-aware parody disguised as an honest attempt. I made it so meta and so self-referential that it instantly frayed the thread to the reality of the intention I set out to manifest – creating a profitable content creator business.

I weaved a story arc in the series that followed in pursuit of my intended path but was doomed from the beginning. I was creating hybrid satire and authentic vlog. This was what me creating content looked like.

My first YouTube video I shot on a more than ten year old Sony camera. I stacked my set with all the objects that represented my fractured creative identity. Snowboards. Guitars. A pastel drawing of a bird-tree-man worshiping a mountain sunset that his life force was attached to. A poster from the cast of the play I directed. My computer for writing and video editing. I narrated my history with each form of expression.

In a way it was healthy to vent about my creative disappointments publicly. A few people saw the video. In truth, I was more pleased with having produced the narrative elements of the episodic story I was setting up than I was with my view counts and subscriber count.

I made a YouTube playlist like it was a season of a sitcom series. The first one only had 5 episodes and presented on themes such as how to dress on your YouTube channel and how to decorate your set.

Then life handed me a new opportunity. I was asked by a friend to shoot a promotional video for her wild horse photography workshop that clients paid thousands of dollars for. It was in California under the eastern Sierra Nevada Mountains. I would get my own horse and tent. All meals included.

I bought $10,000 worth of video gear. I figured I'd start a production company in addition to the content creator business since I already shot videos for work. I disregarded the fact that I didn't like editing other people's videos and that it stole time from my own myth making. I told myself that this wildhorse workshop video would ignite my portfolio.

Days before I left, I had to complete the narrative arc of the beginner content creator. I shot an unboxing video for my YouTube with all the gear I had just bought. Those types of videos were popular and a part of the creator's initiation story. I had to live it all. I thought I might as well check off having made that type of content piece. It was about the act of doing and living it, not making affiliate sales of the gear I recommended.

This was about living the narrative arc. The method actor fuses with the method writer. I was writing my own story by becoming it.

I wasn't just building a business. I was becoming the protagonist of my own script. Would this end in tragedy like my last romance novel had? Or would this be the hero's journey where I live happily ever after?

Chapter 6

Posts and Petroglyphs

I packed the car and set off for California just before the Summer Solstice. My goal was to film the Wild Horse Photography workshop with the new camera gear, shoot content on the way and make it to the Pacific Ocean. I would pick up on the coast where I had left off and turned inland when I moved back to Colorado from Seattle all those years ago. Then I would drive South down the Big Sur Coast where the edge of the continent plunges into the Sea. I'd pass through Los Angeles and on to San Diego to meet my family. They would all be there visiting my sister who lived there now. My first stop was to camp for the night in a canyon in Utah.

I drove into the canyon off the main highway south of Moab, Utah in the dark. I had to work remotely on the way to keep my job and pay for gas which was at its highest record prices ever. Tomorrow, I would work at the Moab public library like I had before when in this area. I had no need to crush 10 hour days driving. I would take my time on this trip and see sites along the way.

There was no cell service in the canyon. I was walled in by ancient slabs of stone. It was mid June and nighttime temperatures were warm at this elevation. I laid a tarp across the rocky ground and set my sleeping bag atop it. Above the lights of the Milky Way shone down upon me.

I sleep the best when I lie upon the ground of our planet. The Earth wraps me in its warm oxygen-infused bubble and holds me out to the stars.

I slept deep and woke to morning birdsongs. Flowers were in bloom amongst small cactus and shrubs. I could feel the expanse of the high desert beyond the canyon walls.

A little trickle of water streamed down the cliffs from the surrounding land gashed with canyons beyond my view. Here was a place where the waters gathered from the higher terrain.

In the middle ran a stream lined with a thin forest of Cottonwood trees. They could only grow in soil beside a stream in this place. I walked into the forest. Baby wild turkeys ran from the brush beside the road. They joined their parents closer to the stream and wandered off into denser vegetation.

I washed my face in the flowing water. Sacred elixir of life flowing in this land of sparse surface water. Upstream an adult turkey flapped its stubby wings as it jumped off a small cliff. It flew over the stream and landed on the other side. It was the first time I had seen a turkey fly.

Ancient peoples who had lived here grew bean, corns, and squash by this stream. It is where the water ran. They raised turkey for the meat and the feathers. They hunted the deer that lived in this desert oasis.

73

After some wandering, I made myself breakfast on my camp stove and then drove a little ways up the road to the site in this canyon I had seen on the map. The one that drew me here.

It was a petroglyph panel made by the ancient peoples of this land between the years 500 B.C. and 1300 A.D.

Pictograph images spanned about 50 feet across and nearly 20 feet high on the cliff face beneath an overhang.

Creatures, magical beings, footprints, and circular shapes were etched into the stone of this desert. These were living stories. There were family and clan images. There were spiritual meanings, calendar events, and tales of hunting patterns. Crop cycles. Spiritual beliefs.

I had read that these images were not just a symbol, but a living spirit being who could act within the world. It was a place the ancient peoples felt was important enough to mark these images in the archives of the Land. Here for everyone that passes through.

The pictographs were living content and this cliff face was the posting platform. To create the content one had to be here and take chisel to cliff and peck away at the stony skin of the Earth. One could only engage with the content if they were here at this place.

This felt more sacred to me than the social media posts we made now. The Earth wore these images as sacred tattoos. These petroglyphs took far more time to create than social media content. The impression it made on you lasted far longer than any piece of viral content that gets drowned out by the endless stream of more and more digital content uploaded daily.

The creators endowed these petroglyphs with spiritual significance that we can speculate upon or interpret for our own meaning. They were meant to last a long time. As long as this cliff face held up against erosion this content would be exposed to the world and all who pass through.

I took my phone out and did a slow pan across the cliff face. Morning birdsong chirped in the background. I didn't film my face or make this a part of my satirical series. I wrote a few words by text to share a message about telling your story from your own perspective then I cut to the slow pan across the petroglyph panel.

I let the images and the location and the sounds speak for themselves.

Chapter 7

The Youtuber in the Desert

I drove to the Moab library and did a day's work. By late afternoon I set out to cross the Canyonlands and journey further West. Heat was upon the Land. I made episodes and Youtube videos along the way.

The series was about the art of the episodic mockumentary and the innocence of playfulness. Though I didn't know it at the time, I was using mockery as a shield against vulnerability. I had to live the experience before clarity came. The emotional journey of the main character Brady C Snow was the experience I sought. The documentation of the episodic journey as social media posts was the medium to seek the knowledge and experience through. I poured myself into it.

I drove further West and filmed myself swimming in a Lava Tube hot spring and then crossed into Nevada. I played the part of a Youtuber making camera gear tutorials in a dried up lake bed. No fresh water or trees in sight. 10,000 years ago this area was a massive lake. Now it was a dusty barren desert lined with barren mountains.

I stood next to a rusted and abandoned car shot up with bullet holes that I would pass by again on my return home when my car would break down. I was Billy the Camera Guy shooting the tutorial for Brady while Brady was out in the desert looking for fossilized fish in the dried up lake bed. I cut to an extra wide shot of Brady in a bucket hat and his lanky legs protruding out of short shorts. He was scanning the horizon with binoculars and looking at the ground with a magnifying glass.

I filmed wide against this barren basin and range country to reveal how small I was as the video tips guy against the landscape. There was shimmering haze in the distance. The mirages danced amongst the blaze of the Sun's photons baking this desert, ghosts of the ancient Lake sending me some message encoded in interpretive dance.

When the tutorial was done I called it a wrap. Another YouTube video in the bag. I drove further into the West of our Continent.

Chapter 8

The Shit Joke that Went "Viral"

I crossed the Great Basin to the Sierra Nevada and met my friend who put on the workshop. With a cowboy hat to shield my face from the blazing sun and to dress the part, I rode a horse out amongst wild horse herds with my video camera. I listened to the Voice of the Land.

The tall Sierra Nevada stood on the western horizon. The White Mountains fortified the eastern front. I witnessed the foals hanging with the herd. The parents forming ranks to protect the young from Mountain Lions. The wild stallions rearing. I met photographers from Europe and America.

I shot *Whats my Nitch?* episodes at the horse corral and from horseback. One of the most viewed TikTok videos from this stretch of the series was one where I spoke in a western drawl about how male stallions make stud piles. They pile their poop up to see who can lay the highest turd on top of the pile. That's the one who gets to mate, I said in my western drawl.

Stallions make stud piles to mask other male's scent and to make their own scent the dominant one. The video cut to me with a roll of toilet paper walking to the outhouse tent the crew had set up. I thought the outhouse was a mirage but then I sat on it and took a shit. The joke was that I was trying to impress females with my poop video. It got good view counts. It was my little temporary cult classic on the Ticky Tok and I pinned it to the top of my profile. Maybe I should have posted it to my dating app profiles.

I shot a serious YouTube video about run and gun filmmaking. I continued the guise of playing Billy the Camera Guy because Brady was more of a narrator and storyteller than someone deeply passionate about video education. Though it was the character Billy delivering the tutorial, it was my own brain's knowledge improvising the lessons. I guess I was trying to prove to myself how much I had taught myself about making videos. It was my best tutorial I could give about how to cover all the b-roll footage and interviews you'd need.

Clouds came over the sun and underexposed my shot for a part of my tutorial. So be it. This was run and gun filmmaking in the great outdoors.

After the workshop I had the footage I'd need to actually edit a promo video for the workshop and a YouTube tutorial about how to film a live event in the great outdoors.

Chapter 9

More Content Experiments on a Trek to the Edge of the Continent and Back

I shot a *What's My Niche?* episode built around a split personality: a modern-day content creator who periodically became a gold-seeking western pioneer. The settlement I established failed to strike it rich with gold and silver so I figured I'd take up mining for oil. The episode cut to me in front of a gas station sign in Lee Vining, California where the price was over $7.00 per gallon.

I said it was too late to get into the oil and gas industry because the oil companies already were thriving so I might as well move to San Francisco and become an app developer. First, I had to be a trail runner and run across the Sierra Nevada Mountains.

I embraced the filmmaker's luxury of controlling space and time. I could make it look like I was running across the entirety of the Sierra Nevada Mountains when in reality I actually drove across them and got out to set up the camera with epic scenery and run into frame in character.

I crossed the Sierra at Yosemite. I recorded myself running the forests and trails along rivers. I ran on high rock outcroppings with views of the mountains. I carried a hiking staff and twirled it in one of the shots.

In another episode shot in the Sierra, I got my foot caught in a boulder and thought I was going to have to saw it off like Aron Ralston, the guy who got his arm stuck between a boulder and a cliff wall. Instead, I twisted my foot free.

The intention behind this was to show that you can dramatize anything in your content.

I found the scat of a pygmy Bigfoot—aka Little Foot—a miniature Sasquatch not to be confused with the dinosaur from *The Land Before Time*, released eons ago during my childhood.

My trail runner character commenced to run across the entire Sierra Nevada Mountains. The episode banked on the art of the montage. I cued "Push it to the Limit" by Paul Engeman. I ran with a hiking staff. I spun it like a ninja and kept running.

The joke was that as a content creator, my goal was to make myself look more badass than I really was. I didn't care if people got the joke or not. The concept was pure mockumentary and what I needed to live in order to process my reality.

The reality was that I had taken up the belief that we had to create a false persona on social media in order to gain financial freedom and make our dreams come true. This isn't true, but I was still in the thick of the content creator experiment playing the protagonist of my own narrative.

The montage saw me run past a view of Half Dome as I descended the West side of the last major Mountain Range before the Sea. I ran through the vast Redwood forests. I tunneled through a fallen and hollowed tree. Then the episode cut to me running up to a view of the Golden Gate bridge in San Francisco.

I threw the hiking staff down and looked into the lens of the camera I held in my hand.

"Well, I made it to San Francisco. Time to get to work on my new app!"

***

I stayed with a former neighbor from Seattle for a night while I was in San Francisco. I shot episodes at my friend's pool where I pretended to be an app developer making an app that locates public restrooms and rates their cleanliness. I gave the narration it my best coding bro persona.

A friend in Denver saw the videos and thought I was serious. She offered to connect me with a developer friend in San Francisco she knew. I had to admit the content was fictitious and I was not really making an app. I was flexing my acting muscle. After only a day or two in the city, my character got annoyed trying to code so I quit and announced I was going to go be a surf bum.

I picked up my road trip on Highway 1 where I had left off all those years ago when I moved back to Colorado from Seattle.

I drove the eroding edge of the continent south. Here the highway clings to the rugged coastline where the Land meets the Pacific. Mountains plummet 4000 feet in a short distance into the churning Sea.

I drove through Big Sur. I hiked up a valley at night and crossed paths with a skunk. It raised its tail and aimed its ass at me but never sprayed. This messenger of the night was a welcome companion on the lonely road.

I filmed episodes as I worked my way south. The series progressed. I made my way down the coast as a van lifer living in a Toyota Sequoia hoping to become a pro surfer.

Off camera, I played with my new Sony, practicing shots and geeking out over depth of field. I practiced rack focus shots with my telephoto lens. I pulled focus from a flowing stream onto the rippling edge of a rapid and was sure to capture the crisp sound of flowing water babbling over stones. I took sunset photos and night photography of the summer solstice moon reflecting on a million waves of the Pacific Ocean there at the edge of my Continent.

South of Big Sur I used the expensive telescopic lens I had bought to film close ups of Elephant Seals swimming, lounging, fighting, and burping. Our media buyer at the company I worked for had been watching my Instagram stories episodes and suggested I use my narrative persona to shoot a comical ad for our company.

I was all in. I shot a comedic ad playing a Steve Irwin type of narrator with my best Australian accent. I filmed myself in front of the Elephant seals promoting our company's software. The premise was comparing the speed of ad idea generation using our YouTube ad library software to the slowness of a lounging Elephant Seal.

When I brought it up to our CEO, he said "let's run ads that will actually make us money."

I was still employed full time during this road trip and had been working week days out of cafes. In Santa Cruz I posted up at a coffee shop and attended a remote work conference. I was signed in on my phone and airpods but assumed I was muted. Their event organizer had accidentally left me unmuted as I ordered a breakfast sandwich and coffee. My dialogue exchange with the barista was broadcasted to the whole event both in-person and remotely.

My coworkers and employer thought it was funny. After the conference, I kept moving down the coast.

***

As I approached Los Angeles I shifted my niche again. Now I was an aspiring actor who planned to audition for the role of Captain Jack Sparrow while Johnny Depp was in his defamation trials with Amber Heard.

Friends from high school and close family got this reference. I had been obsessed with Johnny Depp's Captain Jack Sparrow character in Pirates of the Caribbean as a teenager and young adult. I dressed up as him and impersonated his character for several halloweens in a row and also wore the costume and played the persona at parties. I guess I related to the character of a scrappy pirate who has big aspirations, doesn't quite have his shit together, but improvises his way towards his goals anyway.

In the episodes, I was making fun of myself for thinking I could revive the niche of being Captain Jack Sparrow again. What I was really playing was the aspiring actor trying to make it in Los Angeles, which was something I had once thought I wanted to do.

Being an actor was the first creative obsession I took with me into young adulthood. The aspiring actor trying to make it in Los Angeles was someone I could have very well become in real life if my better angels hadn't been looking out for me. They kept me in love with the mountains and hungry to explore the places outside civilization instead of letting me wander into L.A. where I would have been eaten alive at such a young, vulnerable age by the very agents of lust and malevolent temptation.

I filmed myself stuck in Los Angeles traffic practicing my Jack Sparrow lines, saying I was on the way to my audition. In the next episode I broke into Disney Studios by pulling open a gate to a side entrance and I skipped the line into the auditions. I recorded this at the Torrey Pines golf club resort in San Diego where my family was staying for some conferences my Dad and brother were participating in. The complex looked enough like Disney Studios. I auditioned in a hotel lounge, channeling my inner Jack Sparrow. I still had the flair.

The story picked up speed. I filmed myself getting the callback from Disney Studios. My facial expression changed from one of anticipated elation to dreadful sorrow. I didn't get the part. I broke down crying.

Sublime's 40 oz. to freedom cued. I duct taped 40 ounce bottles to my hands and proceeded to drink away my sorrows. Playing the game of Edward 40 Hands alone would cheer me up from not getting the part.

I chugged from each 40 as Sublime's song played. At sunset, I walked into the ocean and got taken out by a wave. I floated amongst the oncoming waves, bottles duct-taped to my hands, drifting like a castaway. Then I walked out of the sea and cut to a shot of a jet fighter flying over me. The roar of its engine cut the music.

"Oh! I should become a fighter pilot!" I proclaimed.

I had a new niche. The joke was a joke against myself. I was eager to chase shiny new niches and pursue their path to success whole heartedly for a little while before getting interested in something else and moving on. Perhaps this is what souls do as they live through different lifetimes, experimenting. Seeing what feels most true.

In the following episodes I trained outside a naval base fence. I did 5 plyo clap pushups then got up.

"That's good enough for now."

While visiting with family, my Dad filmed an episode for me where I played an aspiring surfer who surfed on a paddleboard. The comedy was corny but I was having fun. I wasn't brooding on perfecting each piece. It was an exercise in produce, release, repeat. Create the piece and then let go and create another.

***

The time came to drive back to Colorado and head into the office to shoot videos for my employer. I shot more episodes for myself on the way.

I drove up a long dirt road to a high vantage point in the White Mountains overlooking the Sierra Nevada mountain range to the West and the vast expanse of Death Valley to the Southeast. Some of the oldest trees in the world grew here. I climbed one of the ancient bristlecone pines for an episode.

The bristlecones are 4000 years old and somehow still grow when 90% of the tree is dead. Though I felt my artistic side had died because I wasn't writing books, making music, or making full fledged narrative films, the 10% of myself that was expressing and creating through these episodes was still alive and thriving.

I made an episode about self care at a desert oasis pool. I demonstrated a skincare routine and got a skin exfoliation by tiny minnows. The minnows chewed at the dead skin on my feet and then it cut to me swinging off a rope and launching into the pool with goggles and a snorkel on.

87

I filmed a YouTube video in a barren desert that was about your content pillars for online business. I wore shorts and my Grandpa's Strike King bowling sunglasses and wore a dusty purple summer flannel. I shot a *Whats my Nitch?* episode that was an ad for water here in the same desert.

"Ah water," I said as I poured some out on a little desert plant and edited in a trickling water sound effect. "Thanks water."

It was my homage to the sacred elixir of life. Most wouldn't notice the spiritual intention beneath the comedy, but it was my little offering. My own way of honoring the water that sustains us.

***

I crossed hundreds of miles to the East side of the Great Basin near the Utah-Nevada border. There at the abandoned bullet-ridden car where I'd recorded my first camera tutorial two weeks earlier, I shot the final *Whats my Nitch?* episode of the trip.

Winds were picking up. Dust devils swirled on the horizons through the slanted light shining through gathering storm clouds. I slouched on the ground against my car with the hood up. The wind howled. I let myself look defeated. I poured myself into this emotion. I acted the scene as a metaphor for my creative life.

I was out of fuel, water, and beer and stranded in a barren desert with only my camera gear working. I took up the camera in my hand and filmed the engine. My dialogue clearly demonstrated that I did not know how to work on cars. I stumbled away into the desert in search of water as the dust storm blew in. Then I collapsed and lay there upon the dried and dusty remains of the ancient lakebed.

Before the sweet relief of death took me, I was visited by EVERY MAIN CHARACTER in EVERY NICHE that I had just played on the last few episodes of *Whats my Nitch?*

The Treasure Hunter, The Western Pioneer, the Trail Runner, the Van Lifer, the Paddleboard Surfer, Captain Jack Sparrow.

Captain Jack Sparrow showed up as the rescuing hero. If Brady was going to take motivational advice from anyone it would be Jack Sparrow.

Captain Sparrow arrives to deliver the final motivational speech to keep me alive. He tells Brady that Brady himself can fix his car on his own. Just as Jack Sparrow sailed a ship through a barren desert without water in Pirates of the Caribbean: On Stranger Tides, I too could ignite the internal combustion engine of my Toyota Sequoia and sail home to Colorado.

Hearing this from Jack Sparrow was all I needed. I woke up with all my energy back. I hadn't found water, but I didn't need it. I had gotten a talking to from Captain Jack Sparrow and all my alter egos. They didn't want me to quit and I wouldn't.

Motivational music cues. I sprint across the desert to my car as the wind howls. I wrap duct tape around a mystery tube and give the camera a triumphant thumbs-up.

I run to the driver's seat. I forgot to close the hood so I run back and slam it shut and run back to the driver's seat. I start the engine and it revs. I had ignited the internal combustion engine of my vehicle!

I set my phone on my camera tripod and position it facing the long dusty road out of here. I hit record, get back in the car and drive the road towards the desolate horizon. Then I stop. I reverse all the way back to the camera. I put it in park, get out and run up to the camera. I look directly into the lens and smile.

"Well, that's almost a wrap!"

CUT!

It was my masterpiece. A full-on narrative epic produced in vertical format for social media. I felt it was my greatest acting, on-the-spot writing, and directing of my entire creative career and it had all been a satire of myself.

My Uncle Craig back in Wisconsin saw my social media story with me broken down in the desert and announced the urgent concern to my Dad and Aunt that I was stranded in the desert. It was the most engagement I had gotten from extended family.

But what Uncle Craig didn't realize was that if I was really stranded all the way out there, how could I have posted the story on the internet?

I told myself I had successfully exposed the raw truth that social media conveys only an altered reality and not the full breadth of one's lore. I had gone to dramatic lengths to demonstrate this.

When I finally made this footage into a full reel, the 4-minute episode had about 266 views on TikTok. I'd broken it into three parts on Instagram. Part 1 had 400 views. Part 2 had 210. Part 3 had 282. That was more than the combined number of people who read my first two novels.

I felt a chapter of my content creator journey had closed. Though I had banged out a fuck ton of content on this road trip, having spent boatloads of money on gas at the time of the highest gas prices in human history, I still hadn't made much money for my fledgling LLC.

I told myself enough playing around. It was time to get serious.

Before I could do that though, my employer wanted to shoot some videos for my job. I had been gone a few weeks. Another acquaintance who owned a catering business in Crested Butte, CO had been seeing my Instagram stories with my video gear the last few weeks and asked me to come shoot a video for his business. He would be the first paid client for my LLC.

I drove back across the vast expanse of the Canyonlands towards Colorado. Instead of turning to the Southwest towards home in the San Juan Mountains, I kept going East to my work's office.

I'd made it back alive. I had spent a lot. But I had footage. Maybe somewhere in all those episodes, I'd catch a glimpse of what I had actually been chasing.

Chapter 10

Between the Reel and the Real

Back in Colorado, I shot new videos for work and filmed an about video for my first paid client's catering company. Before I could get to editing all the footage I shot on the California trip, I had to edit the videos that would get me paid first.

At work, I was editing videos into multiple formats for just about every major platform. I was making ads, organic content, trainings, and managing all our email funnels. I hit my three year mark at the company and I asked for a raise. I had gotten a $5,000 raise each year so far in my salary but this year I was denied. The company was plateauing on its revenue. Even though I was doing more work, my pay stayed the same. I'd been spending a lot on road trips and the video gear. My car needed work done on it.

I edited videos for others, and in my free time I worked on my own YouTube content. I told myself I had to figure out a way to turn my passions for creative expression and playfulness into money.

Crazy videos weren't a business strategy. I needed to build real assets. All the creators said you needed a lead magnet. So I made a Video Shoot Checklist to make sure whoever used it would capture quality footage and audio every time they shot. I made it in a Google Doc and set up an email opt-in form and delivery automation for it. Next I had to promote it.

I made a YouTube video at a waterfall near where I lived and talked about video for business. I dropped a call-to-action about getting the video shoot checklist for free. The video didn't get many views. My lead magnet failed to magnetize any leads for my fledgling LLC.

I was following the strategy my mind told me to – the ones the gurus said to do – while in my heart I knew I needed to be creating something that I enjoyed.

I enjoyed performing and crafting storylines. So in addition to the dry how-to type of tutorials that seemed so unnatural to me, I resumed the *Whats my Nitch?* productions from home, riffing on Brady and Billy the Camera Guy trying to present Brady as some sort of expert in content creation. Billy was getting annoyed with the indecision on a niche while Brady remained playful, easily distracted, and silly. He was more into being a hypey on-camera personality than he was into sharing real value.

***

Now I must confess that I have taken the authorial liberty of writing sequences out of the order in which they actually happened to enhance the narrative effect of this tale.

I took the California road trip and filmed those *Whats my Nitch?* episodes before I filmed the episodes that came before them in the chronological sequence – the intro episodes of the series that I have already given you an account of. Collaging space and time is the filmmakers art and I rearranged the order of releases on social media too.

At this point in my life's timeline none of the episodes had released as reels. They had all been disappearing stories. Everything I've told you earlier about reels performance was after-the-fact reporting.

I didn't like learning new technology when I could continue to get by doing what I already knew. I knew how to post stories. So every minute to 3 minute episode was posted in 15 second chunks strung together with disappearing stories on my nIstagram.

A friend asked me if I really only intended for all those to just be stories and not reels. She said I should be posting them as reels that live on my account forever. I agreed and looked up how to make an Instagram reel.

If I could shoot and edit a YouTube video, use the Youtube optimization tool Tubebuddy, write an SEO appropriate video description, and use YouTube as a lead generation system for my job, I could figure out how to post a reel on Instagram. It turned out that making a reel was quite easy. It was so easy, anyone descended from apes could do it.

I downloaded a mobile editing app and decided the California road trip episodes would not be the first episodes of the series. I would shoot and release prequel episodes to them and work towards them before re-releasing the episodes that I had already shared to my stories as reels, TikToks and YouTube shorts.

That summer I launched the series with my alter ego, the British treasure hunter and Wizard Staff affiliate, as you've already seen. That fall my work took a company trip to Las Vegas where I filmed those "Brady on the loose in Vegas" episodes and received the idea to start a YouTube channel from a brass Eagle in a shop at the Venetian.

I successfully killed and harvested the Elk upon returning to Colorado and brought the meat back to the San Juans. Shortly after I was soaking in one of the many geothermal pools as the treasure hunter of the San Juan Mountains and made my confession that I wasn't really British and that it was time to get serious and start a YouTube channel.

That brought me back to the start of the California road trip episodes I've already narrated. I took that trip and shot that content in summer of 2022. I then shot the introductory episodes as the treasure hunter and the vegas episodes in the fall of that year and released it all during fall and into winter.

At this point it was winter. I had purchased 4 ski passes again which accounted for a decent chunk of my total annual income. My expensive addiction to chasing resort powder was at its peak addiction. I called off an exciting date of someone I had met in real life and not a dating app. I should have probably gone on that date but instead I went off to chase a massive storm forecasted to catch on the Wasatch mountains over Salt Lake City, Utah. I found a cheap airbnb, took my work computer, all the unedited California episodes on my phone, and embraced the road warrior creator within yet again.

This was my creator's myth in motion: even if my reels averaged only a couple hundred views and I still had under a thousand followers.

***

The Wasatch Mountains are biggest around Salt Lake City where the ski resorts are built. This range is narrow compared to most of Colorado's ranges. It's positioned between the Great Salt Lake to the Northeast and Utah Lake to the South so it catches lake effect snowfall. These mountains often stack up some of the deepest snow totals in the American West. With the storm systems crossing vast and dry deserts to get here, the snow that falls is without much of the moisture weight it has when it makes landfall on the West Coast's mountain ranges. The result is light and dry powder, the best for snowboarding or skiing.

I worked mornings and nights remotely from my basement airbnb so that I could ride powder to my heart's content during the days. The liftlines were pretty bad at the resorts, but that's to be expected on a powder day next to a metropolitan area. When work was done I'd edit my California road trip episodes into reels and publish them on Instagram, TikTok, and YouTube shorts. They got me a few new followers.

Friends that saw them as stories messaged me about enjoying California. They thought I was there in that moment. It reminded me how wide the rift is between real life and social media illusion.

Even the big accounts and the influencers and models exploited this ability to make it seem that you were always somewhere cool, doing something exciting. I admitted to them that the reel had been shot 6 months ago and I was actually in Salt Lake city snowboarding. I was not enjoying summer in California.

I didn't have a large following, but a few bigger creator accounts commented on my reels about why they weren't blowing up. I commented back that it was likely the algorithm was confused about my niche and didn't know which audience to make my content go viral to.

It also could have been because my reels were usually 1 minute to 90 seconds long and had narrative arcs with jokes most audiences didn't get. Most the viral content on the platforms was far shorter than that. The popular videos on did not have scenes of dialogue with a story arc spread across multiple episodes.

Viral TikTok content was short, catchy, and easy to imitate. Lip-syncs, dances, or trends. On Instagram, success came from snappy text hooks laid over b-roll, often directing viewers to long captions that kept them reading. The more time spent on the post, the more the algorithm served it to bigger audiences.

Acting absurd scenes, improvising scripts, and creating narrative storylines was not the type of content that did well on social media. I refused to optimize for follower growth. I got new followers and grew the accounts but it was on a small scale compared to the big creators.

I half expected that the episodes would be a hit on social media and it would grow my audience immensely. I told myself I should have started a new account so the algorithm didn't get my niche confused. At that point on my personal account I had engaged with Only Fans models content, nature content, snowboarding content, internet business advice content, and more. Oh well. I didn't want to worry about what I couldn't control and I wanted my original account to attest to the changes in my seasons of life and content.

There were a few of my episodes that got seen by large audiences. A couple of the Johnny Depp reels got a few thousand views. The one that got the most views was not what I would have expected to be my top performer. The reel that received over 20,000 views was the one where I was claiming I'd make a great fighter pilot and planned to enlist in the Navy at age 36.

I guess the algorithm showed it to a bunch of veterans who had a conversation with each other in the comments. They weren't even speaking to me. The algorithm took the signal of many comments as a hot reel and pushed it to more and more viewers.

I had done it. I had accomplished the content creator dream. I had hacked the algorithm and gone viral!

I get why they use the word viral but it makes it sound negative. It sounds like I spread like a disease. Virality was somehow a lot more anti-climactic than people make it out to be. There was no offer or established brand to push traffic to and make money or spread my natural expression. After a few weeks the reel stopped getting shown to viewers.

Vanity metrics wear off fast and we are left with the same hunger for deeper meaning & purpose.

***

Old man Winter kept breathing and the snow kept falling so I extended my workcation in Salt Lake City. A friend back in the San Juans sent me her Dad's contact and said I should reach out and meet up with him. He was a paraglider and it might be something I was into. The idea of flying did sound cool so I reached out.

When I met my friend's Dad he told me tales from his lifetime of flight. He took me to a flight instructor he recommended. They both told me tales of riding thermals of hot, rising air and soaring amongst the clouds. They told me what training to become a certified pilot looked like.

I knew it was the wrong time to take up a new hobby. I had been spending too much on my travels and not saving. I was living larger than my means. My savings were slowly depleting. I had been chasing experience and trying to save memories instead of money. I had embraced the road life. Yet soaring amongst the clouds had me curious.

I asked if I could do a single flight first and then come back to training in the future. The instructor said yes.

I showed up to the flight park on a cold, windy morning thinking this was the plan. Instead of a tandem flight, I got my first solo lesson. I was taught how to kite the glider with my feet on the ground. Then my instructor took me to the bottom of the hill to taste flight for the first time.

The launch involved crouching low and pulling on the lines to inflate the glider and bring it overhead with control. Then you turn and run down the hill. I turned and ran. The glider pulled me up into the air and my feet left the ground. I soared above the ground for a little ways and came to a gentle landing down the hill. My instinct was to cry tears of joy. I choked up but I held it back so my instructor wouldn't see. I had wanted to fly all my life. I had tasted flight and the freedom of being above the ground.

***

Back in the basement bedroom of the airbnb in Salt Lake I discovered a new content creator. Dan Koe. His YouTube videos pitched his free downloads on making genius ideas and it got me on his newsletter. The slogan for it read something to the effect of "join people getting mindfucked every saturday."

Dan spoke about turning your passions and natural talents into a career path. Through the lens of philosophy, he promised that we could do the same. Build a personal brand, productize our knowledge, and earn a living from what we care about.

It felt fresh. Even if the monetization ideas weren't new, the way he framed them landed differently.

Dan preached "you are the niche." I liked this idea. I knew my expenses were getting out of hand with all this powder chasing, airbnb renting, paraglide training, food, gasoline, and the rent I was paying back in the San Juan mountains but I bought his course to learn digital economics and how to make it in the new creator economy.

The course material wasn't any new ideas. It was just repackaged ideas with a different approach, delivered through a new voice of personal experience. After years of fighting and yearning to bring my soul's purpose to the surface, I embraced the idea of fusing business with passion.

The thing was that my passions are diverse and vast. How could I bring them into being in a way that supports my ideal lifestyle?

I stayed in Salt Lake snowboarding, paragliding, working, and studying the solopreneur creator economy for weeks. The time came to get back to Colorado to shoot some video content for my employer. I told the paragliding instructor I'd be back often to continue training since I worked mostly remote. Salt Lake was only six hours from home.

With refreshed hope for financial freedom and a new found drive to learn flight, I made the trek back across the Canyonlands basin. I passed mesas and canyons of eroding Earth where the Colorado and Green Rivers converge and carry the waters of two mountain kingdoms, the Wind River

Range and the Colorado Rockies, toward the Gulf of
California.

***

I had been trying desperately to catch *Whats my Nitch?*
up to the real-time version of me. I reached far back into time
in my phone's expanding digital photo and video archive.
Each edit brought me closer to my present reality. When I
finally released the last episode it was an emotional release. It
was a ton of episodes and hours of footage I had edited into a
narrative arc strung together in what was to me a singular
storyline.

Now I was I finally caught up to the real me. I hadn't
been shooting new episodes for months because I had had
enough to edit. It was a relief to not have to be a content
producing machine.

To shoot in the way I had been with multiple
characters, I had to shoot lines in one camera angle then
reposition the camera to shoot lines of the other character at a
different angle. Then edit it all together. It was a lot of work
and it wasn't making me any money.

The truth was the satire for social media was getting
old, especially if that was all I had to offer. I wanted to create
something of deeper substance. Reconnecting with my flair
for acting had been fun, but I was a one man production team
making fun of myself and the vulnerability I felt in creating
something from the real me.

103

My writing, music, and hunger for collaborative filmmaking was now fully repressed. I was a prisoner of my own fears and insecurities. I believed I had to prove I could build a successful online business before I earned the right to just be myself and create what was truest in my heart.

I had been consuming more Dan Koe. He spoke in a dry, serious, monotone voice with little emotion in his videos. The ideas were his own but renditioned from other creators he followed.

He preached creating content, growing your audience, and making digital products to set yourself free. I wasn't the only one mimicking his voice and message, thinking that was the way to succeed. Dan's content spread like wildfire. Tens of thousands of personal brands sprouted like weeds. Everyone preaching the same thing. Build a personal brand. Grow your audience. Monetize your knowledge.

He said build a personal brand, not build a personal brand exactly how he does but somewhere along the desolate road of overconsumption, the wires got crossed.

I began producing dry videos about content creation and using social media to change your life. It was mimicry of Dan Koe and a total vibe shift from what I had been publishing. I was trying to be serious.

People who had been following the *Whats My Nitch?* series must have though I was either insane or this was some strange part of my joke. I even considered making a separate account just for the dry, copycat business content and keeping my own for personal expression. Yet Dan Koe said you are the niche. Why couldn't I include some educational and inspirational content with the entertainment and bundle all of me up into one personal brand and one account?

I burned hours of free time shooting a bunch of YouTube videos and chopping them into shorts that I sprayed like diarrhea across my Instagram, Tiktok, and YouTube. I worked late into the night on these projects without having any business offer and without growing my accounts by any substantial amount. It didn't take long before I got burned out.

I hadn't published any *Whats my Nitches?* in awhile. Friends started asking about it. Where was *Whats My Nitch?* They had grown accustomed to the frequent releases and now my content was boring and inauthentic. There was a teeny tiny small cult following who wanted to see the series continue.

Even in artistic repression, my creative self was still alive, pulling strings from somewhere deep inside. I hadn't published a book or made new music but I had made all those episodes. They had been my only thread to creative expression at the time.

I had unfinished business with *WhatsmyNitch?* I had left off on episode negative ten while I had been counting up to episode zero. I couldn't leave Brady the content creator and Billy the camera guy hanging.

I ran a poll on my Instagram stories if I should continue the series. The results came in after 24 hours. It was an overwhelming yes. Only one person had voted no. The followers had spoken. I decided to continue the narrative arc.

There were ten episodes remaining before episode zero. I told myself that I'd find my niche by episode zero or die trying.

Episode Zero wasn't just another upload. It was a finish line. A reset point. A symbolic threshold. The moment I could finally drop the burden of the mask and step fully into the version of myself I'd always known was real. To get there, I had to make the most revolutionary *Whats My Nitch?* episodes yet.

***

The *Whats My Nitch?* story line was now about the relationship between Billy the Camera Guy and Brady the Content Creator. It was about the conflict in my mind and soul.

Brady did what he felt. He made videos about using mystix juggling sticks while on a balance board. The joke was that I always switch my niche because the world is an interesting and curious place and focusing is difficult. Billy counseled a profitable niche. He encouraged more strategy and practical execution.

Brady dragged Billy along for the roundabout detour towards finding his authentic niche and made Billy the gruntman. Billy grew increasingly upset and frustrated with

Brady. Billy tried to direct Brady. Billy assumed the niche was teaching people how to be a content creator. Brady made it about his life and being expressive in any way he felt fit.

The negative numbered episodes approached episode 0.

The episodes were a lot of work. The production efforts ate into the time required to actually build a business or create anything meant to live off of social media publishing. I couldn't keep only making satires about myself. I had experienced the emotional journey that I needed to from the fictional representation of the non-fictional me.

I announced to my followers episode 0 would be the final episode.

In episode -2 Brady did a beard tutorial while on the balance board outside on Highway 550 from my apartment in the mountains. Billy got pissed and seized the beard trimmer from Brady's hand and shaved a monkey tail into Brady's face.

A monkey tail is when a sideburn drops to the chin and curls in a line up onto the mustache, across the upper lip and then stops with the other side of the face clean shaven.

Brady did it back to Billy. Billy quit and said he was going to become his own content creator.

"You don't need a cameraman to be a content creator," Billy said.

"But how will I shoot my content?" Brady whined.

In episode -1 Brady and Billy engaged in content creator battles. Billy referred to himself as the Sensei content creator. Brady had shaved a handlebar mustache into his face out of the monkey tail. Since I also played Billy, Billy had a handlebar too. Brady said that rocking the handle bar mustache was his own niche and not Billy's.

They tried to outdo each other in their content. They both went to the same spots in the mountains to shoot their videos. The story arc was set up for the grand finale that I had been waiting for. Episode 0 had arrived.

Episode 0 was 3 minutes long so I broke it into two parts for Instagram. I shot it like a Western duel. I used instrumental acoustic guitar music from the YouTube audio library. I had to outdo the Stranded in the Desert of Nicheless Souls episode. This was going to have to be my best filmmaking yet.

***

Brady and Billy meet in a high mountain meadow in springtime in the deep San Juan Mountains. Each of them wear their camera on a selfie stick slung through their belts. The selfie sticks represent the six shooter of the wild west.

Billy is in the long purple overcoat I wore for the last decade as Halloween costumes. Brady is in a modern hooded jacket and the trucker hat from the show Stranger Things that says "Thinking Cap." Brady sucks on a piece of straw. They both wear a handlebar mustache. Light spanish classical guitar plays in the background.

"Howdy Billy," Brady says.

"Greetings Brady."

They both stand in a wide stance. Hands at their hips. Ready to draw their selfie sticks. The shots are wide. Mountains loom behind them in the glow of the setting sun.

"What's your nitch, bitch?" Brady says.

"Content creation. What's yours?"

Brady removes the straw from his mouth and spits.

"My nitch is content creation."

"That sounds a little broad to me," Billy says. "Don't you think you should niche down even more?"

We cut to a low angle on Brady. The Grenadier mountains are in focus behind him, the setting sun shining alpenglow upon them.

"My niche is actually content creation for creators."

"Well mine is creating creative content creations for creative creators."

"Mine is creative content for content creators who want to create content for other creative content creators and escape their 9-5 job and 5000x their rackflow just by creating content."

"Oh you think you're pretty niched down then don't ya?"

"I do."

"That's fighting words."

Brady takes the straw from his teeth. "We're already at war. Challenge accepted."

A moment of silence ensues as the last gentle notes of the spanish guitar in the song sound out.

Then the music intensifies to a higher paced western duel tune. They each draw their selfie stick and extend their cameras and press record.

They prance about the mountain stage as they each talk to their own camera.

"Whats up guys? I'm Brady Snow."

We cut to Billy:
"Whats up guys its Billy your sensei content creator

Then back to Brady:
"If you want to up your content game..."

Billy completes the sentence:

"...follow my account."

This was my statement that so many content creator advice guys all sound the same.

Brady says:
"I'm gonna be talking about..."

Billy completes the phrase:
"everything you need to know about content creation."

"The creative process!" Brady says.

"Creating content," says Billy.

"Overcoming your hurdles," says Brady.

Billy adds:
"Tips, tricks, tools of the trade!"

We cut to Brady walking with the Grenadier mountains bathed in the glow of the setting sun.

"Become the artist of your own life," Brady says. "But it all starts with your support. Give me that like. Gimme that subscribe, drop that comment..."

We cut to a wide of Billy mumbling to his selfie stick as he walks off a cliff.

As the director of photography of this production as well as the stuntman, I set up the camera on a tripod and then walked off a ledge in Billy's costume. There was a ledge below it that I jumped to as I fell out of frame. I cut to a duct-taped stick figure falling off a different cliff that I filmed at a different time in a different place.

Brady sees Billy's fall and suddenly realizes the severity of his friend's situation. He is no longer in competition with Billy. He must go to his friend who just walked off a cliff while talking to his selfie stick. Brady continues filming with his cell phone and scales down the cliff.

He finds Billy coughing on the ground. Billy says he punctured a lung. He tells Brady that he must go on and keep making content.

"Just don't stop, Brady! Your niche will find you!"

"Okay, Billy!"

Brady breaks down crying.

Playing myself, I got to give my best acting in an intimate close up. I like to think I really showed my emotional range. It was heartfelt.

"Just follow your passions," Billy says. "Your niche will find you."

"Billy, you're the man! You're the Sensei Content Creator!"

Billy looks off into distant space. "I can see the golden light. Heaven is going to be beautiful, Brady, because heaven is full of content creators. Everyone can tell their own story!"

Billy starts slipping from this reality. Pretty acoustic guitar music plays in the background. Billy starts muttering the same phrase over and over. His voice gets quieter and weaker each time as his life force drains from his body.

"Just keep creating content. Just keep creating content... Just keep creating con..tent...."

On his last statement Billy chokes. His eyes cross. He gives his final words.

"Like. Subscribe."

Billy chokes out and dies.

Brady breaks down in a deep cry. It lasts only a few seconds then he swiftly composes himself. He picks up the camera on the selfie stick and presses record.

The sad guitar music changes to the theme song of the show from the original episodes: an upbeat fiddle jig.

"Whats up guys it's Brady Snow and today I'm coming at you to talk about how my best friend just died. He was so committed to his craft that he was talking to his selfie stick as he walked off a cliff. He's going to be inspiring us and me from beyond death. And if you follow my account you're going to be getting all the tools and tricks of the trade about how to create fire content these days."

Brady lights on fire with a visual effect as he says the fire line.

"This is the last episode of *Whats my Nitch?* but I might be making a new show soon. It's called *Nailed That Nitch.*"

I point at the camera and wink as I click my tongue.

The episode cuts here.

This is where I would have rolled the credits and displayed my name in every position and every character of the entire production.

Chapter 11

The Taste of Flight and the Longing for Solid Ground

Even as I wrapped the 'final' episodes of *Whats My Niche?*, I was still trying to make 'serious' content on the side. I mimicked Dan Koe and talked about why social media and personal brands can change your life – even when it hadn't fully changed mine yet. It got boring.

I just wanted to create what was true. What made me happy. I also didn't want my creative fulfillment to come from social media. I had become a slave to the idea of "post everyday to grow." I wanted to return to the idea of sharing when life becomes so rich you *can't help but* share, not because some guru said to post daily.

I knew people who barely touched social media. Their life was rich enough without it. My brother had canceled his Instagram and Facebook and only used LinkedIn and YouTube. There was something more to life than just scrolling and posting. If I was going to share moments or ideas online, it needed to come from a real connection with my natural, off-camera self. Comedy and playful on-camera presence could be a part of it, but I needed to connect with what really lights me up.

That spring I got invited to a vanlife party on the Green River in Utah. Out in the Green River canyon, disco lights were projected on the cottonwood trees and the ancient cliff walls of the canyon. We partied into the night and while everyone slept in their vans, I slept outside under the stars.

On Monday morning I was about to drive to the Moab library to work but one of my new friends lent me their Starlink internet so I could take a zoom video call from her van. After the meeting I jumped into the muddy waters of the Green River for a dip.

Being able to work remotely from anywhere blew my mind. I had been doing this work from the road thing for awhile, but it was always from a town with internet service. Now I was doing it off the grid in a remote desert canyon.

The van life crew hosted another party out on the Salt Flats of Utah. I drove the 9 hours to get there and only filmed what seemed natural and fun. I shot no satirical episodes. We skim boarded the puddles on the flats. The puddles stood upon the flats like pooled mirrors reflecting the sky back into the sky.

After the trip I stayed in Salt Lake. Paragliding continued and I began launching from the top of the hill and ridge soaring, staying up with the wind and flying back and forth along the hilltop. My instructors were not ready to sign off on my P2 license yet, which would allow me to fly solo without being on a radio with a coach.

I was in no rush. I wanted my ability to fly to parallel my ability to create the life I wanted. One where I have the freedom to explore and enjoy life but also a passionate project I cared about. I still believed I had to make a business about helping people get more business. I believed my passions still had to be a separate project only when I had achieved the successful business.

High summer arrived which is the best time to be in the Colorado high country. I spent more time at home and did less flying in Salt Lake.

***

I had been reading the geological history of the mountain range I lived in when high summer arrived. I made reels of my hikes. Always solo and always deep into the wilderness. From the summits I narrated the geological history with the hyped-up kind of energy an influencer would use for their affiliate product recommendations. I pointed out mountain massifs and peak clusters that used to be old volcanoes.

Bushwhacking an off-trail route up and down a different peak, I found the largest concentration of wild raspberries I had ever found. I shot a reel of me eating them, saying "the Bears can't eat all the berries…" followed by me stuffing a handful of juicy fresh wild mountain raspberries in my mouth and chewing.

The nature content with no posting schedule and no pressure to post was nice. I just posted when I felt like it. This was every few weeks at the slowest, a couple times a week at most.

I had managed a few more trips out to Salt Lake for paraglide training but during high summer I wanted to be deep in the San Juan mountains where I lived. A second paraglide instructor that worked with the school I was going through saw my social media posts. In class one time he made fun of me, saying "Brady's been walking."

It didn't bother me because it was where I wanted to be. I knew you couldn't easily fly over these mountains at my skill level because of the extreme topography, unpredictable wind patterns, and limited landing zones. Flying over these mountains I could not bend over and drink from a stream or pick up an interesting stone in my hand. This mattered to me. I was working on my grounding and maintaining solid footing in life at the same time I was learning how to fly.

***

High summer ended as swift as it arrived. One day I crested a ridge after having been backpacking for two days and was met by a cold fierce wind out of the West. It was the breath of Winter sneaking into this Land. That moment marked the end of high summer to me. My activities and my travels changed with the seasons.

It was a matter of weeks before I found myself living out of my car in Salt Lake for a month. I had learned the vanlife ways from my road-dwelling friends. I bought a planet fitness membership and made the Draper, Utah site my primary location in their system. I lived at the flight park out of my car and I kept training on how to fly.

I knew the paragliding was preventing me from working on the creative projects that I felt brewing within. Creative writing and music was building pressure underneath the surface but I couldn't resist the allure of another adventure to chase.

I ridge soared. My instructors launched me at the more advanced flight park. They took me on tandem mountain flights and threw us into wingover spiral dives and then touched down lightly in the grass. They let me launch solo off a mountain from 2000 feet above the landing zone.

The LZ was a school soccer field. I flew down the ridged slope of the mountain soaring high above the solid ground. Beyond in the blaze of the western sun the Great Salt Lake shimmered as a mirror set upon the surface of the barren Earth. My vario began to beep. This was the instrument my instructor clipped to me to sound the alarm when I am in rising air. On the radio he told me to turn.

"Not a granny turn! A sharp turn!"

I was scared of turning too tight. It was an awkward feeling and situation. After a few circles coach came on the radio.

"I think it might be time to head to the LZ now, Brady."

I was losing altitude and he wanted to make sure I'd have enough glide to make my landing zone. I turned and flew out beyond the mountains lowest slopes and over homes, streets and powerlines.

I lined up my landing with the soccer field and the direction of the wind. Over a set of apartments I felt hot rising air. My glider fabric rippled in the heatwind. My vario beeped a little. I flew past my LZ, made one half turn and flew towards the school's scoreboard. Before the board I turned 90 degrees left into the wind, glided, and set my feet down with a soft landing.

"That was the coolest thing I've ever done in my life," I told the other paragliders in the field.

I was happy to have my feet back on the ground and feel the stabilizing gravity of the Earth.

I had over 80 flights. Only 35 were required for my P2 license, but my coaches kept students longer to ensure advanced skills became muscle memory. I didn't mind — I wanted my ability to fly to parallel my ability to live.

I had more training to do.

They launched me at the Northside flight park into big air. Here you soar a steep bench of upsloped land covered in sagebrush and steep gulleys. You're near houses and within close proximity to the highway. The method here is to stay up with the rising air and land where you takeoff instead of at the small landing zone at the base of the steep hill. Anywhere else down low was not good for landing. There was a barbed wire fence containing a pond. There were buildings and out beyond it all there was the city and the highway.

The goal is to get high enough out front and then turn downwind where you double your ground speed. Then you send it back to the high ridge behind the take off zone. There you typically find rising air compressed by the steep hillside and it takes you up nearly a thousand feet above where you took off. They called it benching up. My instructors wouldn't sign off on me in the training until I did that.

You soar in the flight pattern with lots of other pilots in the air. There's plenty of room but on days with low wind, people scratch for lift. Everyone wants to bench up. I had been doing passes out front, coming in for a landing, touching down and then keeping the glider controlled in the air above me, walking to the lip of the downslope and launching again.

I was taking a break with the glider down from the air to talk to my coach. As I stood there we noticed commotion in the air above us.

A hang glider and a paraglider were entangled and plummeting down to the Earth. A reserve chute went out but it was too late. The gliders and the pilots hit the ground. Crowds rushed over. Coach got on the radio and told the airborne pilots it was time to land because a helicopter would be coming to fly the injured to the hospital.

Everyone came in for a landing. I spoke with some guys who had ran to the crash scene. It was a tandem paraglide flight with a expert pilot flying a passenger, a woman who was flying for her first time, and a hang glider pilot from out of town. I got the name of the paraglider pilot.

I met a man who was on edge and hadn't heard who the crash victims were yet. He was saying how he hoped the pilot hadn't been his instructor but the names matched. I broke the news to him.

He was distraught and said the pilot had a family and had been building a house. He was a good pilot. All I could say was I'm sorry and I hope for the best.

Later that night I found out the tandem paraglider pilot had died. He left a wife and several kids. The passenger was taken to the hospital for critical care. I never found out what happened to her. The hang glider pilot spent a night in the hospital and then left without severe injury.

I was spoken to by my friend's dad about this. He said anything could have happened. The sun could have gotten in the pilot's eyes. He said people can get greedy when the wind is light and everyone tries to bench up. He had witnessed many deaths in this sport over several decades of flying. He said he witnessed one guy crash who had been coherent and speaking then moments later died, his aorta having been severed on the crash.

This mid air collision and death hit me hard. I had been so close to it. I had been flying in the same airspace moments before it happened. I was reluctant to fly there again and was wary of air traffic but I still flew the next day. The wind was too light to bench up. I was okay with that. The fact that I was flying at all was a miracle in itself. I also had no need to rush my flying. I had enough to figure out about my life with my feet on the ground.

***

After a month in Salt Lake prioritizing flying, it came time to once again return to Colorado. I told my instructors I'd be back to continue my lessons. Before I left I looked for housing in the city, thinking I should move here. I found a house with a couple close to the paragliding park and the entrance to the canyons that led to the ski resorts. I told them I would move in in December.

When I returned across the high desert to Colorado I had to go straight to summit county to shoot video with my employer. I had been gone awhile and he needed videos. The business was losing money fast. Google had made a targeting policy change that affected the use case of one of our primary softwares.

Customers were canceling their monthly subscriptions. Competitors with the same kinds of products were firmly entrenched in the market and the new offers we had worked hard to put together did not gain traction.

On the way to the office I passed through Grand Junction out on the western edge of the state line with Utah. Traveling 70 mph on the highway East there is only a brief window in the Land where the southern horizon drops low enough to behold the San Juan Mountains. It was nearly dusk when I passed through. I saw them standing in the amber alpenglow of the setting sun. I felt a sense of nostalgia.

Those were the mountains I had been calling home the last 2 and a half years even if I had been on the road a lot. They were my spiritual sanctuary and my anchorpoint connection to my love for this Planet. Something in that sunset struck a chord deep within me. Deep down I knew I couldn't abandon them and move to a big city again. Not yet anyway.

I drove further East and the mountain tops dropped below the horizon. I drove into the coming night to make it to work the following morning, commuting yet again out of the vast distances of the West.

***

Back in the office before we shot some ads and content, my employer confronted me about my move to Salt Lake. I had told him as a friend that I was looking into it. He revealed to me the full details of the business's health. He said he had been paying people's salaries out of saved money and that the business was losing money. He had already had to let the COO go and he said he may have to let me go soon too.

He said no hard feelings if I looked for another job. Instead of accepting the need for a new job to continue my lifestyle, I told him this would light a fire under me to finally figure out how to get my own business plans off the ground.

I was too proud to let the idea of being solely self sustaining for the sake of more freedom go. We shot some content and then I drove back to my mountain sanctuary. It was October.

By December he said he had to let me go. The conversation was quick and to the point. If we had been on a pirate ship like the job felt like at times, the conversation would have gone like this:

"We're out of grog and the profits from raiding ports has been down," Captain would have said. "We have to let you out on this remote island, without any supplies or grog."

"It's okay, Captain. It's about time I commandeer my own ship and become my own Captain anyway," I would have said.

Then I turned in my weapons (the remaining videos I had edited for them) and stepped off onto the Island. Only in real life, the island wasn't a tropical isle but a remote apartment in the deep mountains. Captain let me keep the work computer though. The laptop I used to make all my longform video edits on.

I canceled the move to Salt Lake. I had been almost certified to fly but I knew there would be more expenses to keep up with the sport afterwards. I declared my flying on hold until I found a better way to live my purpose with my feet on the ground.

I was actually relieved. As great as flying was, it came with high risk that required lots of time devotion to stay on the top of your game. There were things on the ground I had yet to accomplish. Devoting so much of my time and money to the thrill of flight without having accomplished what I was called to on the ground yet just didn't feel right. Without a solid foundation on the ground, I knew I wouldn't be able to sustain the flying safely.

My pursuit of adventure and thrill were an important part of me but it was not my complete being. My devotion to it was preventing me from creating and exploring other parts of myself.

I had forsaken my curiosity to share myself on a deeper level. I craved early morning writing sessions. Meaning in a long term project.

Getting laid off for the first time in my life from the job that funded all my travels & adventures was the Universe redirecting my focus inward, toward what I had been repressing. The Director of Content role had given me a lot: experience, knowledge, and a glimpse of how a small online business really worked.

I had tasted location freedom. Immense schedule flexibility. I had experienced firsthand what operating a small, online business was like and the strategy and work required behind it. My employer had given me a taste of that life. I had lived it for three and a half years.

I had clung to it because it gave me the illusion of freedom. When the foundation crumbled beneath me, I realized I was going to have to adapt now. I was going to have to slow down and feel. I'd have to cut back on my traveling lifestyle, at least for now, and root down in the San Juan Mountains. I had to be brave and face that reality.

My finances had taken a hit. Yet the deeper danger was that my soul was on the line.

Act III

Let the Niche Emanate from the Soul

Chapter 12

The Library within the Caldera

The town of Silverton, Colorado north of where I had been living at Purgatory sits in a deep mountain-ringed valley on the edge of an ancient volcano that grew up inside of another volcano. They don't look like volcanoes these days but they once spewed lava and ash. Today they are a conglomerate of densely packed mountains.

The original volcano emptied its lava chambers over a million or more years and collapsed in upon its hollowed remains. Then the next Volcano sprouted up inside of it. It erupted and flowed lava, making new land, and then it too spent its load and collapsed on itself.

Over 30 million years or so glaciers and rivers carved valleys out of the original shape . I witnessed a similar spectacle on Mount Saint Helens once while I lived in Washington. I stood on the horseshoe shaped rim of what had once been a higher cone-shaped volcano before May 18th, 1980. I climbed 6000 vertical feet up it and stood and gazed at the new cone pulsing and smoking in the crater below.

These volcanic remains around Silverton, CO were done erupting and had created the space and the volcanic soil for new environments to grow. Glacial ages carved the calderas up and carried loads of sediment out into the surrounding lands and towards the Sea. Over thousands of years the forests spread into these remains. Animals moved into the deep valleys. Ecosystems took shape.

New phases of growth don't look like growth at first. The old constructs and support structures need to come crumbling down to make room for what is to come. For me, I had to lose the remote work freedom to create the terrain for the new era of life to take shape on.

I had to break my travel and thrill addiction even if temporary. I had to temper my spending habits. I had to stop frantically dashing across the Lands of the West and root into place for awhile.

It would not be forever but for a little while it was needed to get my creative rituals down again.

The money stress was real. It was an excruciating time to have to assemble the employment puzzle because my focus had been on my creative rebirth and I had been trained to believe being an employee was bad. Making a profitable business that can replace your salary while also reviving your creative habits at the same time is no easy task.

I had enough savings to live off of for awhile. I applied to jobs and did a little marketing freelancing but it all seemed so monotonous and contrary to my creative intentions. It may have to be that way in life sometimes – doing one thing to pay bills and another to feed the soul – yet I still felt my priority was to work on the one I had been neglecting the most.

I went through Julia Cameron's Artist Recovery program in her book "The Artist's Way." Her program worked wonders. I started to write in the mornings again before doing any employment tasks.

Every morning I would set my computer upon the dawn altar, my coffee table, and face the rising sun in the East. I tried to be writing every morning as the Sun rose above the ridgeline of the West Needle Mountains out my window, coffee steam rising from my mug.

I began writing a book that told the story of my struggles and travels in adulthood. Three themes took root: creative striving, my romance with the Land, and the pursuit of the Cosmic Lover Incarnate. The content creator niche exploration had been a more recent part of the larger tale.

I began to see each challenge or setback I had experienced as necessary to my inner growth, rather than as negative experiences that happened to me that I could never recover from.

I worked on rewriting the mantras I lived by. It's true what the self-help gurus say. You can rearrange your mindset and habits. We can reprogram the neurological network in the brain from one of cynicism and scarcity to enthusiasm and abundance. We can accept the past but work to create a more fulfilling future.

It doesn't happen overnight though. Once I committed to the process, the times tested my patience and my mindset.

***

At this time a soulmate entered my life. The Gods sent her as a different species – not as a human lover or business partners– but a creature of fur and breath.

My neighbor had a husky up for adoption named Katana. I watched her for an evening to see how it felt. After I had returned her after the trial, Katana found me the next day She emerged from the woods along Highway 550 after she had ran away from her off leash training with my neighbor.

She came right up to me and let me bring her back. I was unsure about taking on the responsibilities of a dog, but she had chosen me. I was lonely and we had a strong connection.

We took a final test to see if we were a good match. Some friends and I took her backcountry touring in some of the first snow of the season. We took her into the caldera within a caldera. We went to the outer western edge of the inner caldera as the first snowstorms had started building the season's snowpack.

At the top of our route Katana gazed off into the mountains like I do. There was so much more to discover out there in that vastness. She knew it too. When I snowboarded down she ran right behind me, galloping through the powder. She left her pawprints in the snow-draped slopes upon the remains of the caldera rim.

I adopted her. The companionship was good for me. She needed lots of exercise and I needed lots of walks in the woods and mountains. She had high energy and loved exploring the terrain.

We were a perfect match. The soul companion had been sent.

***

As the snow fell and the snowpack deepened, I did more than just snowboard. I continued writing the book and processing my past. All the pain and all the joys.

I took a break from posting on social media all the time. I put the *Whats my Nitch?* episodes on hiatus and I rarely published reels. It felt good to not have the pressure of posting all the time and only posting when I wanted to.

I took action to maintain control of my focus. I unfollowed the models. I got off the dating apps. I became more intentional about what content I consumed and when I did it.

For the first time in years I balanced my love of snowboarding with other meaningful practices. Writing. Picking up the guitar and just playing for fun. I wrote a new song about an old rusty nail in a haunted house. It was a metaphor for being rusty at your creative habits, but committing to do it anyway to bust off that rust.

I received download after download from the fabric of spacetime on what my soul's work was. It came at an expense of a draining savings account to have this luxury of reflection time but it was what I needed most.

I felt the delicate nurturing of my creative rebirth was too vulnerable to subject to the job application process. I guarded it with ruthless legions.

I didn't want to waste emotional stamina grappling for the attention of faceless gatekeepers of salary and benefits who were working online living in cities far away and unaware of what the weathers were doing over the San Juan Mountains. An instantaneous new marketing job wasn't going to solve the bigger problem anyway — that my creative ritual had been forsaken all these years and I had been neglecting my soul hygiene.

Perhaps a new fulltime remote job would make sense someday but for the time being I had to confront my inner turmoil. I had too much to process from the cacophony of data my consciousness had collected the last many laps around the Sun.

I didn't know what it was yet but there would be a way to pay for my survival and still do my soul work. It would take time to figure out.

Knowing what we don't want and how we can set boundaries in our personal lives is a huge step. We never know until we walk the wrong path for a ways.

As winter deepened, I went about my new rituals. The volcanic soil from past eruptions had settled upon the weathered remains. The terrain primed for new growth.

***

By spring my memoir had encompassed more than the last decade of my life. It was over 90,000 words. This book you're now reading is under 40,000 words. The bigger memoir was more than twice this one's length – wrought in rants of raw and unfiltered personal essay and veined with moments of scene and poetic burst.

As I caught up to the present the memoir became harder to write. To end a memoir when the timeline is still in motion is a challenge.

Not even the writer can stop time. They can give the illusion of freezing time on the page but as the narrative time stands frozen the Sun keeps orbiting the black hole at the center of the galaxy, pulling the Earth in its orbit along for the ride.

The long orbit around the black hole exposes the pages to floating dust. As long as the Earth keeps in motion our DNA coils continue their slow unraveling. This process of aging. The words written by the writer warping in meaning as the planet enters new sections of our Sun's 225 million year orbit - the cosmic year.

I chose to end the memoir with my morning sunrise writing ritual. It had become the most important part of my day. If I didn't do it, I had failed.

I painted the scene with words. Me at my writing shrine in my mountain abode facing the sunrise over the mountains.

I thought this was an appropriate ending. It was not some big event like marriage or sudden wealth acquisition demonstrating my external success. It was about the collapse of the structure that had been keeping me caged and my revived dedication. The return to the soul journey. The shift that had happened was about creative return and emotional restoration.

My first novel had ended with a sunset. My first memoir ended with a sunrise.

I put the final words on my book and called it complete. It was a six act book coming in at roughly 90,000 words (more than twice as long as this book).

I went from ready to publish to not wanting to publish in a matter of weeks. I felt it was still too raw and vulnerable to release. Being witnessed on such a deep multi-dimensional level while still in the act of transformation seemed like torment.

My book spanned many themes across more than a decade of my life. I had needed to write it for my own clarity.

I considered the idea of taking a singular theme from the more recent years of it and writing a shorter book. Something more direct and relatable for others. Yet I couldn't front the cost for a massive hiatus and hibernation to write a whole book again even if half its length.

The planet had tilted its northern hemisphere back towards the Sun. The first green shoots reached up from beneath the melting snow. Spring had sprung and it was time to return to the world of work.

I acquired a consistent weekly video client through a vanlife friend. I edited their YouTube vlogs on DIY home construction. It wasn't enough to live on but it was consistent money going into my business account like I had wanted.

I decided to get a job in addition to the client videos. I was still needing a hiatus from digital marketing. I wanted to feel what it was like to have an in person job rooted in the local community of this mountain range. Not the edge of the foothill settlements but the inner mountain range kind of folks.

I wanted to feel what it was like to get paid for presence and not just going through the motions of doing the work while my mind and soul were elsewhere.

***

I drove North on highway 550 into the remains of the Calderas. I went to Silverton, the only town in San Juan county in the core of the mountain range. I dropped a resume off at a saloon from the 1880s. It was a resume for a bartending job with experience in project management, email marketing, and video production. I got an interview that day with the owner and he offered the job.

137

I spent much of the summer telling tales of the mountains from behind the bar. I spoke of my own personal treks, the geologic history, the mining history.

One summer day a geologist came in for a beer who had studied the volcanic origins here. He described how the mountain cluster north of town surrounded by more mountains had been a volcano that grew inside another collapsed volcano. Just south of town there was a scar in stone where a glacier dragged a boulder across a cliff face over thousands of years. This was my kind of workplace conversation.

In July the flies swarmed the bar. The owners equipped us with a pump-action salt shotgun to kill the invaders. This was the best part of the job. I'd stalk the flying multi-eyed aliens and wait for them to land. Then I'd blast them with salt from point blank. The guests cheered me on. This was the kind of western saloon they had come for.

There was something sobering and grounding about working with physical matter over digital content. Moving the matter of liquids and solids around was grounding. Bottles and the devils drink muddled with soulful human conversation. It wasn't a salaried job or a $100k a month automated recurring revenue but it was enough to live on in my sanctuary in the San Juans while I did the work needed to dig my soul out of the hole I had buried it in.

I needed to feel human connection again. Something real. Yet even at the end of each closing shift, after everyone had left, I'd pour myself a drink and sit at the bar. I gave a cheers to the ghosts that entered the saloon and drank the beverage down amongst their company before heading home.

***

As fall approached and tourism dropped with the incoming winter, I knew I'd need another job. Another bartender was a teacher at the local school. She said they needed someone who spoke Spanish so I applied. The translation, interpretation, and teaching skills I had done over a decade ago in Gunnison were in high demand in the school system within the Calderas.

They had a nice library with big windows that faced Kendall Mountain in the East – the debris and detritus of the volcanic flows. They had a large map of the world. A place to get your bearings and be reminded of the importance of place.

I got offered the job as a part time gig with benefits so I could keep working on the client videos and any projects of my own. I found a nicer 2 bedroom apartment than what I had for only 50 dollars more per month. I moved into the town nestled between the ancient Calderas.

I was isolating deeper in the mountains but I had always wanted to live here. The location would allow for less social distractions. The allure of backcountry snowboarding and hiking in my favorite land would be there but I would be able to partake of that medicine when I needed it.

The rawness of the landscape and the new responsibilities and rituals stripped me down to my essence. Only from that place can the slow growth of new ecosystems take root.

***

I strolled often along the banks of the Upper Animas River that was two blocks from my home. This waterway had been called the River of Lost Souls by the first Spanish explorers.

As the nights grew cold I harvested the last of the wild chamomile from the field along the river and made tea.

Winter drew near. I stacked firewood in the wood shed.

The Northern Hemisphere of our Planet tilted away from the Sun. Winter deepened. The days got short and dark.

I made fires in my woodstove. I lived the simple life and became clearer on all my tasks than ever before.

I had three projects in the works. One was the video mini-course. The safe bet and an exercise in offer building. The last act of the narrative arc I had yet to complete.

The other project I gave myself permission to develop slowly. This was to organize a framework for aligning my life's tasks with what I feel in my soul I am meant to do. The things

140

I had been aching for but still felt the conditions of life were to scarce to support. I had to find a way to bring them to life.

Orbiting the outer fringes of those gravitational bodies, my raw creations were explored as experiments and grounding exercises. I extracted one of the 3 themes from my grand memoir I wrote the winter before and began turning it into a mini-memoir that became this book.

I played guitar sometimes and worked on new songs. I wanted to create from overflow, not from a need to be validated by my creations. I created to release. I released to free up space for greater presence and to nurture new growth into being. I did this living here in the moat between the rims of the Calderas.

The Land was its own library. Archived stone and the timbers of the ages were stacked for me to study at will with my dog Katana.

***

I honed my skills in simplifying. I learned to cast aside shiny new ideas and focus on small achievable tasks instead of trying to win the entire war in one single, decisive battle.

I made time to write, snowboard and play music.

I designed a simple framework I could follow to get clear on what activities, habits, and tasks really mattered in my life. I outlined a simple guided journal around my framework on living a more fulfilled life rooted in purpose. The journal outlined the six life categories that our soul tasks fall into: Survival, Health, Relationships, Play, Mental Fitness, and Creative Ritual.

I wrote journaling prompts and clarifying questions for each category. They were designed to shine light on the tasks and obstacles standing in the way of soul bloom. I decided I wanted to share the prototype version with the world and improve it over time.

This would be my slow bloom project. I released the first draft digitally. I could iterate and expand in time. This was the right approach to building something. Make a base version, what the business guys called a minimum viable product, and expand and build over time.

I kept building the video business offer. I wasn't chasing freedom through hustle. I was moving towards freedom through release. This was a part of the journey and not the full route. On the mountain trek this was the off-trail part where I had to bushwhack through dense brambles. Yet even the most densely grown thicket reveals a way through when we slow down to listen for the path.

By spring I had the offer stack and the foundational content YouTube videos. I also had harvested an answer. This building of the solopreneuer business model was not the catalyst to freedom as so many of the gurus had promised. It was not the final destination and never had been. It was just an obstacle on the path that I had to climb over.

This project had been the final illusion. The idea that we had to package and monetize ourselves to be free. In truth, success was being true to who we were.

I had tried on many niches like I had access to a massive Hollywood wardrobe.

The satirist. The personal brand builder. The video coach. The scrappy creator. The man chasing freedom through hustle. Each one taught me something and none of them fit for long because each one was me trying to fit into a form that did not use my natural voice.

I had chased treasure like a pirate of the creator economy. I had followed the self-declared gurus into the field like the rogue mercenaries who swore they'd raid the Spanish fleet and bring gold back by dusk.

Yet dusk always came and the gold never did.

If financial success had come about by these tactics as quickly as promised, I now know it still wouldn't have been the solution to the void I felt. No amount of treasure replaces the feeling of remembering who you actually are.

The true wealth, the thing we're all trying to remember, isn't monetary.

It's not scalable.

It's forged like a crystal. Under darkness. Over time Through pressure.

I had made the course modules, the coaching offer assets, the websites, the email automations. I could promote it now. Yet I knew from the depths of my soul it was not what was going to fulfill me. Even if I worked at it until it paid ALL the bills and more, the content messaging would still be misaligned with what I needed.

I don't let go easily. Pivots often take awhile. I had to release the educational video tips content. I had to finish following the script. I had to prove – even if just to myself – that if my soul didn't fit the model, maybe the model didn't fit all souls. I had to prove that suppressing the inner calling to chase the money was not the answer to happiness and fulfillment. To repress and ignore the soul's calling for the pursuit of profits was folly.

I had to prove this by making myself suffer through the wrong niche one last time. The last act of the method writer writing plot twists for the method actor.

When we become aware that the tasks and intentions are misaligned, we can pivot if we choose to.

We adapt.

Not all effort is in vain for we have learned something through the struggle.

***

Growth is not a straight line. It is a spiral. We come back to the same places and situations with internal change before there is external proof of change.

Can we thrive in abundance doing our soul's work? Or must doing our soul's work be an additional struggle against the demands of survival?

Survival has always been hard. The toils of hunting, plant gathering, water gathering, shelter building made it hard to create beyond those needs. Yet mankind invented agriculture and there was a blossoming of arts and crafts. Pottery. Basketweaving. Rock art. Astronomical insights. Storytelling. Advancements in technology.

There are many in this world who have not forgotten how to express. Tribes gather to perform their communal dances and carry on the traditions of their ancestors. Artists, musicians, and writers create their works of art and release them to the world.

Why is it so hard for so many of us to let our most natural self exist? To let our soul's flowers sprout? How can we find purpose and identity in a digital world?

We must confront our shadow work. We must look at what is uncomfortable and painful about our experience in life and accept its existence. Only when we can sit with that shadowbeast in the darkness can we move through back into the light of our days.

We are still deserving of joy and meaning even while we are within the process of our becoming.

***

I flicked the lighter and lit my stack of paper and cardboard. The flame spread and I added kindling to the young blaze. I blew gently on it to fan the flames.

Outside the temperature dropped below zero degrees Fahrenheit.

I fed larger pieces of ponderosa pine to the flames and the wood caught.

I sat at my hearth and watched the small fire I had just created to heat my home from the inside against the winter night at 9,300 feet in the Rocky Mountains.

Within the dancing of one fire's flames you can see all the fires our ancestors have comforted themselves beside throughout the ages.

Before homo sapiens, the modern human, our ancestor homo erectus, used fire 1.7 to 2 million years ago, sheltering in a cave against the bonecold winter nights.

We lit fires and burrowed beneath a larger mammal's hide.

For ages upon ages, all we had to comfort our minds was the companionship of others and the stories we told each other around these fires.

Today, we have the smart phone and wireless internet. We have electric heating and stoves. The modern era is a new age that takes a lot of electricity and computing power to distribute the wealth of information and blossoming spiritual awareness that humanity has inherited.

After we discovered agriculture and made permanent settlements it became easy and common to stray from our soul's purpose. The creature comforts comforted us so much that we forgot that we each have a unique gift to share.

We now have the opportunity to reconnect with ourselves and build something unique and rewarding to each of us.

In the end, it turned out "What's my niche?" was the wrong question. More appropriate questions would have been "how can I structure my life to engage all my passions in balance? How can I best offer my gifts in service to others?"

I couldn't think my way there. I had to feel. I had to live it. The answer wasn't a niche. It was a feeling.

Let your transformation be wrought by your emotional shift, not your external validation. The strategy and the plans fall into place with emotional clarity and alignment with purpose.

The ponderosa logs catch fire and produce the blaze that will heat me through the night and into the light of the risen sun. I close the iron door to my wood stove and sit back in my camping chair beside the hearth.

My phone vibrates with some alert. I ignore it. I open my macbook pro and my writing document. The flame crackles. The wood pops.

I feel the bubble of heat expand outward. With this comfort and this heat I begin to write.

The subtle scent of burning ponderosa keeps me focused. Grounded. The clicks of the keys on my laptop and the roar of the flames in the stove are the sounds of self aligned to soul. The auditory proof of trust in the process. Allowing time and intention to work its magic.

Outside my windows the distant stars burn their ancient fires. Inside my mountain abode between the Caldera rims my hearth roars distant thunder.

The thunder sounds like its rolling away somewhere in the vast night over the mountains in the East. In the direction the Sun will rise.

Whats My Nitch? Renewed for a New Season

I was high on a peak above the surrounding valleys. This was the first time I made a tentless camp above the timberline on a new moon, a night without the comforting glow of the full moon. It was just me on the crest, the mountain holding me up to the stars like an offering from the Earth.

I saw the silhouette of the jagged skyline to the West, the rim of the ancient Supervolcano Caldera in shadow as the daylight faded to the glimmer of the Milky Way and the feint blue glow of the atmosphere, our planetary energy shield.

In the other direction to the Southeast lightning flashed. I glassed that southeastern horizon with my binoculars and beheld the flashes of lightning casting momentary shape to the outer volcanic field's eastern mountain remains.

I could smell the stones of the mountain. A sharp smell like pulverized dust laced with ancient micro crystals. This storm was far away and I could not hear its thundering. I would be safe here to pass the night on the edge of the precipice. A safe route down dropped away into the basin to the South. I laid back and bundled into my sleeping bag, capturing the heat emitted from my mortal body. I would need it this night.

I thrust my nose into the cosmos. The ripe fragrance of Milky Way dust tickled my nostrils.

Though I beheld the stars of my galaxy from this mountain top my gaze drew inward to a memory beyond this lifetime. I saw the expanding effulgence of this milky spill of stars spreading across fathoms of depthless dark. I saw vast volcanic cones gathered together upon an expansive mesa domed up from a nearby sea. Glaciers came and went many times. Each visit they engulfed the region and sheathed the landscape in ice and then receded. Every time they left they took the debris and detritus of stone with them and reshaped the landscape, carving deep troughs and sharp peaks amidst the once conical volcanoes.

I passed the night in this way, sleeping some, waking often to gaze into the timeline of existence.

At sunrise, I put my phone on my selfie stick, extended it and pressed recorded. I held my arm outside the sleeping bag to film myself waking up. I threw the sleeping bag off of me and rose with high energy.

"Good morning from 13,000 feet!" I said.

I hear a voice beside me on the peak.

"Do not force the content creation, Brady."

I turn to see the ghost of Billy the Camera Guy standing before the San Juan Mountains. Behind him, the

150

Grenadier Range stands tall and sharp, stone fins rising from the magma sea of the molten inner Earth.

Billy wears a green robe. A belt is around his waist with a selfie-stick with a clear phone case set in it. His hair is back in a pony tail, and new thick rimmed glasses are set upon his face. A blue aura glows around his body like a constant charge of flowing lightning bolts.

His advice echoed in my mind: do not force the content creation, Brady.

"Really?" I ask. "Is it my intro?"

Billy emits a blue glow from his body.

"Don't be so eager to BE a content creator. In essence let your content create itself through the force of your own passion," Billy says as he opens a clenched fist. "Only then can you become one with the force of content creation."

"Should I say something more exciting like 'Hey hey look at me, I'm on a mountain! Haha!'"

I flail my legs and hands outward as I say this, trying to give my best attention-grabbing performance.

Billy responds in a tone as calm as the breeze flowing over this mountain.

"Enough with that for now, let's try the selfie-stick extension."

"Okay," I say.

I brace for the selfie-stick extension. I grab the end of the stick and extend it quickly to its maximum.

"Too jittery," Billy says.

I try again.

"Too rushed," Billy says.

"A little chiller? Just be calm?" I ask of my Sensei Content Creator.

"Take a breath. Feel the force of these mountains flowing through you, and then try," Billy says.

I take a breath and then extend the selfie-stick. I speak directly into the camera.

"So I'm Brady Snow and I talk about creativity, content creation, and manifesting your dream life."

I smile into the camera and give a thumbs up. Then I close the selfie-stick and the phone falls out to the ground.

"Shit!" I say and look to my Sensei. "How was that?" I ask him.

"Not bad, not bad, coming along Brady," Billy says as he claps.

Billy pulls out his own selfie-stick and the clear phone case with grace. He extends it and speaks directly to his spirit cell phone.

"This is Billy the Sensei Content Creator and today we are in the mountains where I died. I walked off a cliff talking to my selfie-stick. I am back as a spirit and I am here to instruct you all on the art of content creation. Everything I learn I pass on to Brady so make sure you follow his account too."

Billy keeps the camera rolling but looks off into the distance. He points at the distant terrain.

"Oh, you can see that cliff I walked off over there."

I squat on one foot and hold the selfie-stick under my legs, trying to get a trick shot. My phone falls off the selfie-stick.

I project subtitles on the screen...*New Episodes Coming Soon.*

When I look back to Billy he is gone. It is only me, my selfie-stick, and my phone all the way up here where the Land meets the bluebird sky.

I decide to shoot a short reel to share my joy of being here.

I set my camera on the tri-pod and film a wide shot of my peaktop camp. Uplifting acoustic guitar music cues. I exit my sleeping bag and stretch as words pop up on the screen: *When you wake up on a mountain…*

I make a jump cut to me doing morning yoga to the words *Do your wake up routine…*

I cut to me dunking a tea bag in a jetboil thermos and sipping as I gaze into the distance. The words on the screen say
Take a Look to the South.

Take a Look to the North.

I turn and look in the other direction.

Look East.

The frame cuts to me on a different part of the peak sipping tea with one hand, then bringing binoculars to my eyes with the other.

I cut to a closer shot on me looking through the binoculars.

Look West, the words narrate.

The camera cuts again to me stretching with tea and binoculars in my hands.

Text pops up:

Only to realize you've already accomplished all your goals for the day.

The camera pans around my mountaintop camp. My sleeping bag is laid out on my pad that is set on top of a blue tarp. My gear is sprawled out here at my makeshift home.

The lead guitar slides into the rhythm and I cut to the view from camp at sunset.

The camera pans out across the landscape.

Orange alpenglow reflects on the peaks and the remaining patches of snow. The sky beyond the mountains is a blend of yellow, orange, and pink. There are no clouds in sight. The camera pans into the sun riding low over the jagged horizon. An orange bulb of a solar flare blossoms in the frame as the camera comes to rest on this final image of the day.

I turn the camera off and put the selfie-stick away. I sip my tea and gaze off into the mountains I call home.

Reviews Appreciated

If this book resonated with you, I'd love to hear your thoughts. Honest reviews help independent authors like me reach more readers and continue creating meaningful work.

Leaving a review only takes a minute:

1. Go to Amazon.com

2. In the search bar, type "What's My Nitch Brady Snow"

3. Click on the book and scroll down to Customer Reviews

4. Select Write a Customer Review and share your thoughts

Thank you for taking the time to leave a few words. Your feedback helps this work find the readers who need it most.

More Stuff from Brady Snow

Cosmic To-Do List Journal
Use my guided life-design framework to clarify the habits and tasks that matter most for a fulfilling life.

bradysnow.com/cosmic

Other Books by Brady Snow
Find my novels, memoirs, and future works here:

bradysnow.com/books

Newsletter – Lore of the Soul
Personal reflections, essays, and updates on new creations.

bradysnow.com/newsletter

YouTube
Explorations in creativity, purpose, and the natural world.

Also watch former episodes of *What's My Nitch?* under my playlists.

bradysnow.com/youtube

Instagram
Follow along to see what I'm up to at:

www.instagram.com/bradycsnow

Works Cited & Referenced

Google. *Google's Gemini AI Model 2.0*. Google, 2 Jan. 2025, https://www.google.com. Accessed 2 Jan. 2025.

"Niche." *Oxford English Dictionary*, Oxford University Press, https://www.oed.com. Accessed 20 Dec. 2024.

Rubin, Rick. *The Creative Act: A Way of Being*. Penguin Press, 2023.

"How Stories Connect and Persuade Us: Unleashing the Brain Power of Narrative." *NPR*, 11 Apr. 2020,

https://www.npr.org/sections/health-shots/2020/04/11/815573198/how-stories-connect-and-persuade-us-unleashing-the-brain-power-of-narrative. Accessed 6 Sept. 2025.

"Storytelling Is Good for Us — And Our Bodies." *Psychology Today*, 9 June 2021,

https://www.psychologytoday.com/us/blog/the-stories-of-our-lives/202106/storytelling-is-good-for-us-and-our-bodies. Accessed 6 Sept. 2025.

"Social Media Usage Statistics." *DemandSage*, https://www.demandsage.com/social-media-users. Accessed 6 Sept. 2025.

"Social Media Usage." *Backlinko*, https://backlinko.com. Accessed 6 Sept. 2025.

"Social Media Statistics." *University of Maine,* https://umaine.edu. Accessed 6 Sept. 2025.

www.ingramcontent.com/pod-product-compliance
Lightning Source LLC
Chambersburg PA
CBHW021146090426
42740CB00008B/963